Who I Am
in
Jesus

Who I Am
in
Jesus

Sarah Hornsby

Published by
√ chosen books

FLEMING H. REVELL COMPANY
OLD TAPPAN, NEW JERSEY

Scripture quotations are from:

The King James Version of the Bible

The New American Standard Bible, copyright © The Lockman Foundation 1960, 1962, 1963, 1968, 1971, 1972, 1973, 1975, 1977

The New English Bible, © 1970 by the Delegates of the Oxford University Press and the Syndics of the Cambridge University Press

The Holy Bible, Revised Standard Version, © 1946, 1952 by the Division of Christian Education of the National Council of the Churches of Christ in the United States of America

Library of Congress Cataloging-in-Publication Data

Hornsby, Sarah.
  Who I am in Jesus.

  1. Jesus Christ—Prayer-books and devotions—
English.   2. Devotional calendars.   I. Title.
BT306.5.H68   1986   242'.2   86-22021
ISBN 0-8007-9087-1

A Chosen Book
Copyright © 1986 by Sarah Hornsby
Chosen Books are published by
Fleming H. Revell Company
Old Tappan, New Jersey
Printed in the United States of America

This book is
dedicated with gratitude to:

Andy and Tish Anderson
for forty-seven years of parenting
and to
Robert and Jo Hornsby
Jim's parents, and so also mine
for twenty-five years.

A special gracias
to each person mentioned in this book
who lived with us through the decision
and determination
to leave a comfortable college pastorate
to live and build with the poor
in German Pomares, Nicaragua.

To those Nicaragüense
who always seemed to give us their best
so freely and with such love
who face incredible poverty
and the raging of nations
with day-by-day courage, faith, sense of humor
And to Rafael,
whose story weaves like his music
and my prayers
through it all.

Contents

Thanks to the following who read this book and helped me have the courage to share it:

my husband, Jim
our son Andy
Faye Inlow
Carolyn Mosley
John Roush

Thanks to the editors, Jane Campbell and Ann McMath, who polished the rough edges of my anguish to produce a smooth stone.

Note:

In the original draft of this book, I included many vivid illustrations of the power of God at work here in Nicaragua, as well as specific stories of my own struggle over a variety of issues. In order to conserve space and fit into a uniform format, the editors felt it necessary to eliminate many of these from the text. Though I am sorry that I was not able to convey to you the depth of our experience here, this puts the responsibility on you, the reader, to write your own adventures and struggles with unedited detail, as you use this book. God may lead you in paths you have not chosen and could not have anticipated, but He promises to be with you in the fire.

To the Reader:

This book is primarily designed to aid, to encourage, to challenge you in your daily times of conversation with our heavenly Father. As such, it is a daily devotional guide. But it is more. It demonstrates a style of dialogue in which our energies, our frustrations, our preoccupations are honestly exposed to the light of God's cleansing power and thus focused more clearly to be useful in announcing the Kingdom of God. Inevitably, this guide contains material very personal to me and in some ways records my own spiritual journey during the time it was written.

My husband, Jim, our young son, Matthew, and I are living and working in a rural, poverty section of Nicaragua. Here we build houses with teams of local families and help develop Christian leadership through Habitat for Humanity.

Here I struggle with political, interpersonal, sexual, and religious conflicts—things not normally shared in devotional guides. These are things, however, that each of us confronts at times, things that must be shared honestly with God if we are to grow according to His plan and realize some measure of the effectiveness He has in store for us. We must grapple with them if we are to discover who we are in His Son, Jesus.

It is my hope that you will share with God the conflicts and joys of your environment, your specific daily preoccupations. I long for us all to appropriate the energy and peace that come from oneness in Christ so that we can see His government established in our hearts and families, and in our nation and world.

Here are some suggestions on how to use this guide fruitfully:

1. Look up the Scripture passage for the day and read the meditation for the week. Read the verses several times, in different versions if desired.

2. Do a word study on key words using *Strong's Complete Concordance* or some other good reference book.

3. Take time to meditate on this Scripture's application to your situation as an individual and citizen of a nation.

4. Write down your thoughts and form a prayer of the questions and desires of your heart.

5. Picture God's presence, His light, peace, love, surrounding you. Listen, expecting Him to direct your thoughts and give you insight. Write down what you believe He is telling you.

6. Ask yourself if these thoughts are consistent with Scripture and, if applied, will produce the fruit of the Spirit.

7. Periodically share the writings with a trusted pastoral friend.

8. Act in obedience to God's voice.

Who I Am in
Jesus

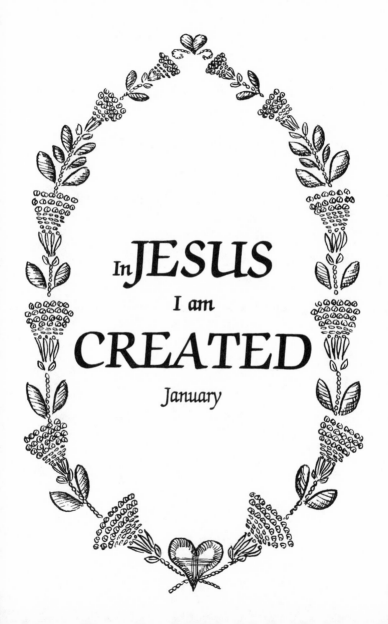

In JESUS
I am
CREATED

January

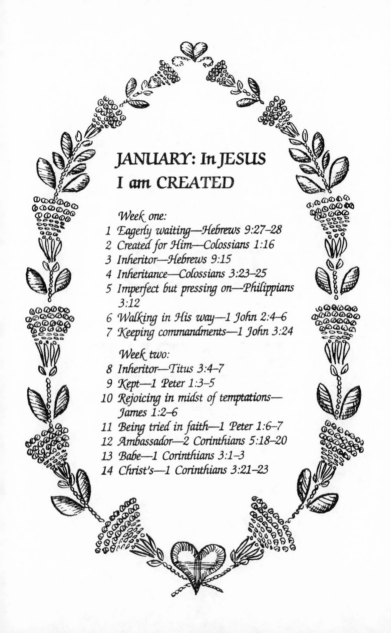

JANUARY: In JESUS I am CREATED

Week one:
1 *Eagerly waiting—Hebrews 9:27–28*
2 *Created for Him—Colossians 1:16*
3 *Inheritor—Hebrews 9:15*
4 *Inheritance—Colossians 3:23–25*
5 *Imperfect but pressing on—Philippians 3:12*
6 *Walking in His way—1 John 2:4–6*
7 *Keeping commandments—1 John 3:24*

Week two:
8 *Inheritor—Titus 3:4–7*
9 *Kept—1 Peter 1:3–5*
10 *Rejoicing in midst of temptations— James 1:2–6*
11 *Being tried in faith—1 Peter 1:6–7*
12 *Ambassador—2 Corinthians 5:18–20*
13 *Babe—1 Corinthians 3:1–3*
14 *Christ's—1 Corinthians 3:21–23*

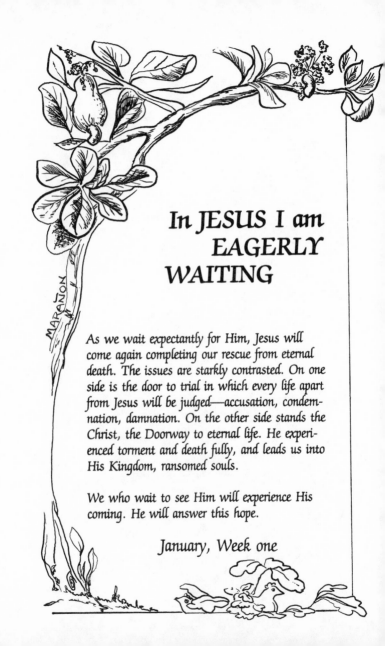

In JESUS I am EAGERLY WAITING

As we wait expectantly for Him, Jesus will come again completing our rescue from eternal death. The issues are starkly contrasted. On one side is the door to trial in which every life apart from Jesus will be judged—accusation, condemnation, damnation. On the other side stands the Christ, the Doorway to eternal life. He experienced torment and death fully, and leads us into His Kingdom, ransomed souls.

We who wait to see Him will experience His coming. He will answer this hope.

January, Week one

Father, I love it when Your Word comes alive to me. Awaken me so that in everyday relationships others will see the possibility of living in You, of walking in Resurrection life.

My child,

I rejoice when you are on that cutting edge where faith dispels the darkness of unbelief, and love drives out hate. There is no place in the universe that is untouched by My glory. No heart is too cold to remain unwarmed when touched by the flames of forgiveness. Though all will not respond to you, it is my nature in you to keep burning. . . .

"And as it is appointed unto men once to die, but after this the judgment: So Christ was once offered to bear the sins of many; and unto them that look for him shall he appear the second time without sin unto salvation."

Hebrews 9:27–28, KJV

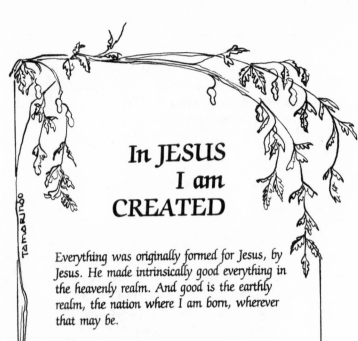

In JESUS I am CREATED

Everything was originally formed for Jesus, by Jesus. He made intrinsically good everything in the heavenly realm. And good is the earthly realm, the nation where I am born, wherever that may be.

Father, these words exhilarate me. I grew up with a sense that America was the number one nation in the world, the blessings of wealth lavished on us because we are a "Christian" nation. Yet when I weighed my preconceptions against the lifestyle of Jesus, I could never be comfortable with them.

It is healthy for me to be in Nicaragua. Here I am overwhelmed by the generosity of those with so little. Here I appreciate Your abundance— cotton, rice, bananas, coffee, sugar. Yet, I grieve

January, Week two

that when natural resources are exported, these hard-working people are left in poverty. Still, I have seen vibrant, lively faith in many people here. Help me shed every vestige of old prejudices.

My child,

My Word reveals My Lordship and love for all people, for every place. As you comprehend My authority—even though you feel terrible anguish over the suffering due to greed and evil in the world—you will rejoice in the fullness of what I have planned for individuals and nations.

"For by him were all things created, that are in heaven, and that are in earth, visible and invisible, whether they be thrones, or dominions, or principalities, or powers: all things were created by him, and for him."

Colossians 1:16, KJV

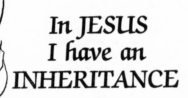

In JESUS
I have an
INHERITANCE

In everything I do, I want to be motivated by love for the Lord. My life is directed by intimate relationship with Him, not by trying to please other people. Thus I know that my inheritance from being His child will be received in full. I am sure of this because He owns me utterly and I seek to serve Him as a slave in bondage to a good master.

By the same token, when I am involved in unjust actions morally, physically, or socially, when I injure or offend anyone, then I will receive punishment because God has no favorites.

Father, I think of the motive behind our being here in Nicaragua. It is a positive action of love in a place where many people have been hurt by certain policies of my own country. It has been hard to witness that hurt.

—— January, Week three ——

Moses interceded for his people as if he were part of the problem. So did Elijah. Jesus wept over Jerusalem and gave His body as part of the answer.

My child,

when you are in the stream of My love, you are often called to give up your life. Even now you have found inexpressible joy from meeting Me in brothers across the barricades made by men.

"And whatsoever ye do, do it heartily, as to the Lord, and not unto men; Knowing that of the Lord ye shall receive the reward of the inheritance: for ye serve the Lord Christ. But he that doeth wrong shall receive for the wrong which he hath done: and there is no respect of persons."

Colossians 3:23–25, KJV

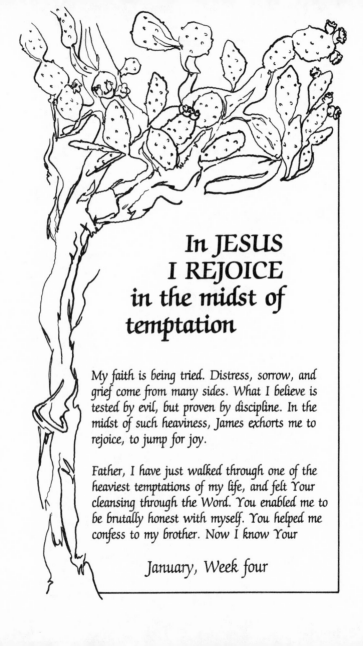

In JESUS I REJOICE in the midst of temptation

My faith is being tried. Distress, sorrow, and grief come from many sides. What I believe is tested by evil, but proven by discipline. In the midst of such heaviness, James exhorts me to rejoice, to jump for joy.

Father, I have just walked through one of the heaviest temptations of my life, and felt Your cleansing through the Word. You enabled me to be brutally honest with myself. You helped me confess to my brother. Now I know Your

January, Week four

healing. Now I can rejoice, jump for joy! The songs come from my depths. Songs of trust and praise.

Only in You, O Lord, are all things possible.

Gracias, Gracias, Señor, for Your cleansing, Your forgiveness, Your mercy.

My child,

I turn your mourning into dancing, your passion into compassion. In Me is no evil that cannot be changed into good. Nothing is too difficult for Me to overcome when you give it to Me.

"My brethren, count it all joy when ye fall into divers temptations; knowing this, that the trying of your faith worketh patience . . . If any of you lack wisdom, let him ask of God, that giveth to all men liberally, and upbraideth not; and it shall be given him. But let him ask in faith, nothing wavering."

James 1:2–6, KJV

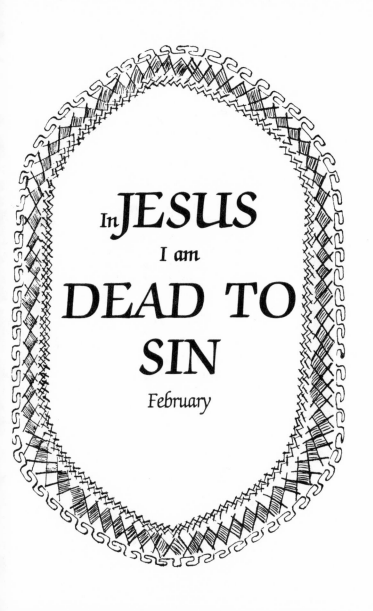

In JESUS
I am
DEAD TO
SIN
February

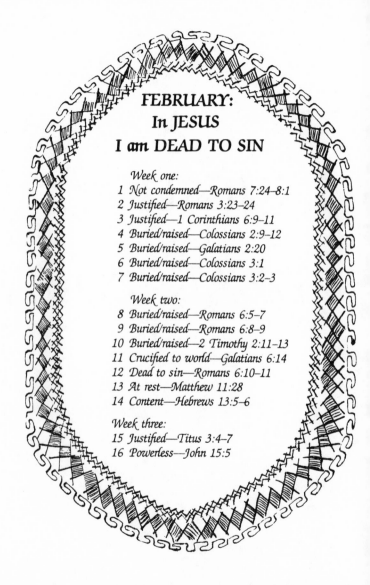

FEBRUARY:
In JESUS
I am DEAD TO SIN

Week one:
1 *Not condemned—Romans 7:24–8:1*
2 *Justified—Romans 3:23–24*
3 *Justified—1 Corinthians 6:9–11*
4 *Buried/raised—Colossians 2:9–12*
5 *Buried/raised—Galatians 2:20*
6 *Buried/raised—Colossians 3:1*
7 *Buried/raised—Colossians 3:2–3*

Week two:
8 *Buried/raised—Romans 6:5–7*
9 *Buried/raised—Romans 6:8–9*
10 *Buried/raised—2 Timothy 2:11–13*
11 *Crucified to world—Galatians 6:14*
12 *Dead to sin—Romans 6:10–11*
13 *At rest—Matthew 11:28*
14 *Content—Hebrews 13:5–6*

Week three:
15 *Justified—Titus 3:4–7*
16 *Powerless—John 15:5*

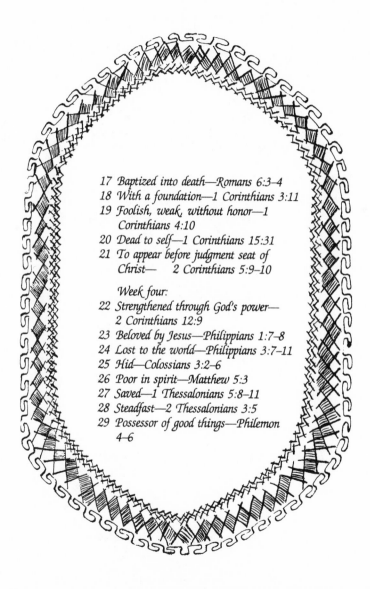

17 *Baptized into death—Romans 6:3–4*
18 *With a foundation—1 Corinthians 3:11*
19 *Foolish, weak, without honor—1
   Corinthians 4:10*
20 *Dead to self—1 Corinthians 15:31*
21 *To appear before judgment seat of
   Christ—   2 Corinthians 5:9–10*

Week four:
22 *Strengthened through God's power—
   2 Corinthians 12:9*
23 *Beloved by Jesus—Philippians 1:7–8*
24 *Lost to the world—Philippians 3:7–11*
25 *Hid—Colossians 3:2–6*
26 *Poor in spirit—Matthew 5:3*
27 *Saved—1 Thessalonians 5:8–11*
28 *Steadfast—2 Thessalonians 3:5*
29 *Possessor of good things—Philemon
   4–6*

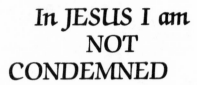

In JESUS I am
NOT
CONDEMNED

The penalty for our evil actions and sinful natures is removed from us when we are united with God in Jesus. In His love we no longer fear punishment for our crimes. In His life we are no longer damned. Hallelujah!

When we first came here Rafael was unable to accept forgiveness because he had not overcome his desire for alcohol. At one time he had worked as a lay minister in the Catholic church, and after a fifteen-day binge with alcohol, he was too humiliated to return to work and chose to set aside his calling.

Jim and I have patiently loved him, and now he desires to take the place God has for him, even if it means not drinking with his friends.

February, Week one

This resolve has been a wonderful tension—a three-way balance between God's forgiveness, our belief in him, and his own courage.

Jesus, what You did begins to sink in. In the tenderness of Your love for Jim and me, for Rafael, and every other sinner, Your death paid that final cost. In You, death and hell are defeated.

My child,

when I paid the price for your life, I did not mean for you to be burdened down again with the weight of sin and guilt. Come quickly to Me. My outstretched pierced hands reach for you to embrace you, to comfort and encourage you to walk in My footprints of love.

"There is therefore now no condemnation to them which are in Christ Jesus, who walk not after the flesh, but after the Spirit."

Romans 8:1, KJV

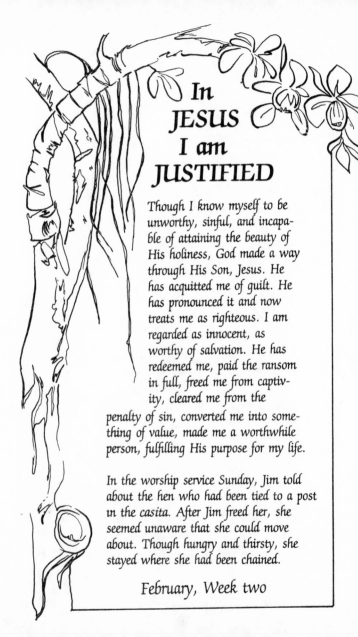

In JESUS I am JUSTIFIED

Though I know myself to be unworthy, sinful, and incapable of attaining the beauty of His holiness, God made a way through His Son, Jesus. He has acquitted me of guilt. He has pronounced it and now treats me as righteous. I am regarded as innocent, as worthy of salvation. He has redeemed me, paid the ransom in full, freed me from captivity, cleared me from the penalty of sin, converted me into something of value, made me a worthwhile person, fulfilling His purpose for my life.

In the worship service Sunday, Jim told about the hen who had been tied to a post in the casita. After Jim freed her, she seemed unaware that she could move about. Though hungry and thirsty, she stayed where she had been chained.

February, Week two

Many things can be chains binding us, but we need to recognize our freedom and exercise it. Let my focus be on You, Lord, on what You have done rather than on my own failings and inability to make things right.

My child,

freely I have forgiven you. I have given you My love. Freely receive and freely give.

"For there is no distinction; since all have sinned and fall short of the glory of God, they are justified by his grace as a gift, through the redemption which is in Christ Jesus, whom God put forward as an expiation by his blood, to be received by faith."

Romans 3:22–25, RSV

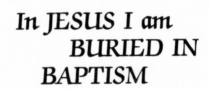

In JESUS I am BURIED IN BAPTISM

I am buried in baptism and risen with Him by faith. In the ceremonial act of baptism, I am absolved of past sin and guilt, overwhelmed with His forgiveness, fully drenched with His love. The old "me" is interred spiritually with Jesus in the grave. The strong energy of God brought Jesus from His corpse, from sin and disease, from the violence of the religious right and politically expedient, and from the grief that killed Him.

Conviction of the truthfulness of God, reliance upon Jesus, and constancy and fidelity to this assurance act as a channel for me to rouse from spiritual death in company with Him.

Last night I went into my bedroom, and through the concrete block wall I could hear a love song playing over and over. I knew that in the bedroom next to mine were two single men and

February, Week three

one voluptuous woman, the director of the school. They were laughing.

They are my family here. How to relate? How to awaken spiritual desire in them?

My child,

immorality is worldwide, a pit of death dug by animal passions. You have them, too. They are My gift, and yet must be used to bring forth children of My making rather than providing a night's pleasure.

As you share the best I give you—assurance, belief, fidelity—as you demonstrate My compassion, caring, and forgiveness, a hunger for the spiritual will awaken, not in all, but in some. Believe Me, it is worth going through hell to enable even one to come home.

"Buried with him in baptism, wherein also ye are risen with him through the faith of the operation of God, who hath raised him from the dead."

Colossians 2:12, KJV

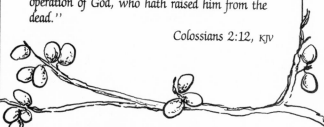

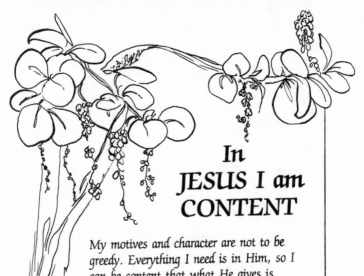

In
JESUS I am
CONTENT

My motives and character are not to be greedy. Everything I need is in Him, so I can be content that what He gives is sufficient.

I wondered why so few people take Communion in the Mass held once a year in German Pomares and discovered that others do not go because they do not have money for special clothes for the service.

This same vanity about clothes keeps many from marrying in the church; a white wedding dress costs more than a year's salary for the average worker. This explains the large number of common law marriages.

Father, I'm grieved to learn that Celestino, one of the young men living here with us,

February, Week four

is not married yet has a new baby. His common law
wife has three children by another man. He has three
children by another woman. Yet Pastor Randy Bremer
said recently that 83 percent of marriages in the U.S.
are adulterous, so who are we to judge?

Help me be fair and not to impose impossible cultural
restrictions on others, yet speak the truth in love.

My child,

My job is to convict and convince. Your twenty-five
year relationship with Jim will speak an important
message. Your honest questions and heartfelt caring for
each one can open doors to a better way, without a
threshold of condemnation.

"Let your character be free from the love of money,
being content with what you have; for He Himself has
said, 'I will never desert you, nor will I ever forsake
you,' so that we confidently say, 'The
Lord is my helper, I will not be afraid.
What shall man do to me?' "

Hebrews 13:5–6 NAS

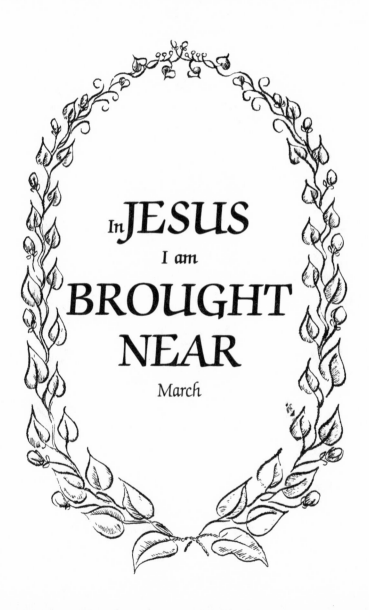

In JESUS
I am
BROUGHT
NEAR

March

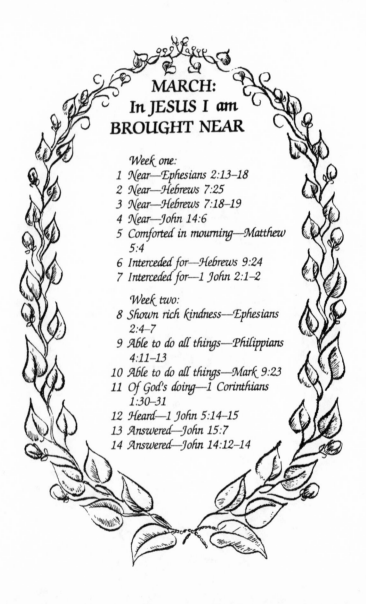

MARCH:
In JESUS I am BROUGHT NEAR

Week one:
1 *Near—Ephesians 2:13–18*
2 *Near—Hebrews 7:25*
3 *Near—Hebrews 7:18–19*
4 *Near—John 14:6*
5 *Comforted in mourning—Matthew 5:4*
6 *Interceded for—Hebrews 9:24*
7 *Interceded for—1 John 2:1–2*

Week two:
8 *Shown rich kindness—Ephesians 2:4–7*
9 *Able to do all things—Philippians 4:11–13*
10 *Able to do all things—Mark 9:23*
11 *Of God's doing—1 Corinthians 1:30–31*
12 *Heard—1 John 5:14–15*
13 *Answered—John 15:7*
14 *Answered—John 14:12–14*

Week three:
15 Answered—John 16:23–24
16 Answered—Mark 11:23–25
17 Confident—1 John 2:28
18 Confident—Ephesians 3:11–12
19 Confident—Hebrews 4:14–16
20 Believer—1 Peter 1:20–21
21 Confident—Hebrews 10:19–25

Week four:
22 Bold—Ephesians 3:11–12
23 To be judged—Romans 2:16
24 Power of God—1 Corinthians 1:22–24
25 Wisdom of God—1 Corinthians 1:24
26 Partaker of Communion—1 Corinthians 10:16
27 Confident—2 Corinthians 3:4
28 Recipient of power—Ephesians 1:19–21
29 Part of priesthood—1 Peter 2:4–5
30 Saved with joy—1 Peter 1:3–4
31 Adopted son—Galatians 4:6–7

In JESUS I am
BROUGHT NEAR

At one time the Gentiles had no hope of drawing close to God. Only the Jews were given the way of cleansing through sacrifices, the way of truth through the Law. They alone had the joy of being claimed by God as His children through circumcision and the observance of Sabbaths, feasts, and festivals.

Then came Jesus, the perfect Son, the perfect sacrifice. He is the way, the truth, the life. He is the fulfillment of the Law, our joy! His blood, the blood of God poured out, brings us close to the Father.

Father, blood is being poured out daily by warring governments. Much blood is shed in Your name, but is not Your nature. How can I be close to You when I feel as a North American that this blood is on my hands?

March, Week one

My child,

when the Israelites sinned, the intercessor Moses prayed for forgiveness. When the blood flowed from Jesus on the Cross, He said, "Father, forgive them."

You are to intercede for all nations and give your body as a living sacrifice.

My hands reach out and grasp yours. Gently by My blood I cleanse and free you from this guilt. I strengthen your hands to demonstrate this compassion to all who suffer from poverty, and to all who suffer from power.

"But now in Christ Jesus you who formerly were far off have been brought near by the blood of Christ."

Ephesians 2:13, NAS

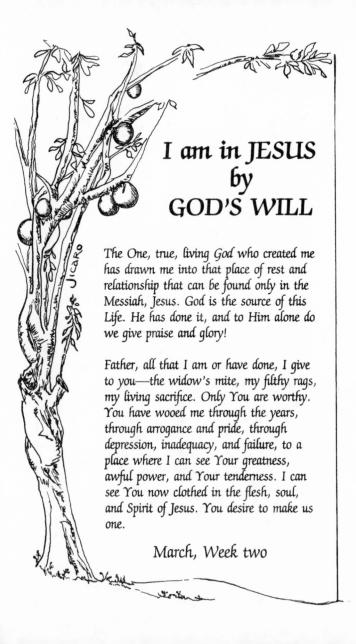

I am in JESUS
by
GOD'S WILL

The One, true, living *God* who created me has drawn me into that place of rest and relationship that can be found only in the Messiah, Jesus. God is the source of this Life. He has done it, and to Him alone do we give praise and glory!

Father, all that I am or have done, I give to you—the widow's mite, my filthy rags, my living sacrifice. Only You are worthy. You have wooed me through the years, through arrogance and pride, through depression, inadequacy, and failure, to a place where I can see Your greatness, awful power, and Your tenderness. I can see You now clothed in the flesh, soul, and Spirit of Jesus. You desire to make us one.

March, Week two

My child,

see what I have done through yieldedness in others. I delight in expressing Myself through the infinite variety of persons I have created. When you yield to Me and enjoy My creating and loving through you, this expression will be unique and produce a harvest of joy!

"But by His doing you are in Christ Jesus, who became to us wisdom from God, and righteousness and sanctification and redemption, that, just as it is written, 'Let him who boasts, boast in the Lord.' "

1 Corinthians 1:30–31, NAS

In JESUS I have SALVATION JOY

In the Resurrection of Jesus, I have a lively hope, a certainty of my inclusion with Him in the happiness of eternity. God is worthy of adoration and praise for His generous compassion.

He has birthed in me, quickened in me, expectation and confidence in His plans. What He has given me as His child is pure forever, guarded by His power.

Father, in the dark this morning I heard shots and was disturbed not knowing where they came from. Then I heard the resonant, steady beat of a snare drum. People were walking along the dirt road beside our house singing of You, the heavenly Father, and I realized it was a celebration.

As I went out to watch, the group moved on down the road, singing. The celebration had to do with the purity of Mary, the virgin.

March, Week three

On a morning like this it seems good to praise You for these people who have watched through the night and boldly proclaim Your name as the sun rises. Thank You for lifting the veil of darkness that accents our differences, and keeps us from knowing how perfect You are. Awaken hope in us till it springs forth in the brilliance of day.

My child,

when you clothe yourself in the robe I give my prodigal, you will look on all others who love Me with holy respect. You will appreciate what has caused them to be different. As you understand and welcome them, they will know that they have found a stepping stone into My promises.

"Blessed be God . . . who according to His great mercy has caused us to be born again to a living hope through the resurrection of Jesus Christ from the dead, to obtain an inheritance which is imperishable and undefiled and will not fade away, reserved in heaven for you."
1 Peter 1:3–4, NAS

In JESUS I am an ADOPTED CHILD

and heir of God. Because this is true, God has sent His breath—the living Presence, the Spirit of Jesus—into the center of my being, into my thoughts and feelings. He is calling out to get my attention. He entreats me to recognize and receive God as Father, Daddy. No longer am I a slave in bondage and subjection. Now I am a sharer in all my Father possesses. This intimacy is my necessity.

Father, I recall You told Joshua to go in and take the land. You spoke through Paul that I am to cast down strongholds of evil within me and within society.

Thank You, Jesus, that I have authority over temptations. I have the authority to discover Your will, and to intercede with power.

March, Week four

Last night the moon was full and gleamed silver, illuminating the world below. The sky filled with clouds and reflected that glory. Despite threatening news reports and the fear in all nations of war, of hunger, of disease, I know that You are Lord. Somehow I play a part, and it is not too hard.

My child,

you know intuitively the prayers that are straight from My heart. As a swimmer parts the waters with ever more skillful strokes and moves evenly to his destination, so you are to draw near to Me by your life of prayer. My Spirit will buoy you when you are weary. He will propel you to the goal—releasing that spirit of love into the world.

"And because you are sons, God has sent forth the Spirit of His Son into our hearts, crying, 'Abba! Father!' Therefore you are no longer a slave, but a son; and if a son, then an heir through God."

Galatians 4:6–7, NAS

In JESUS
I am
ALIVE
April

APRIL:
In JESUS I am ALIVE

Week one:
1 *Recipient of wisdom—*
   1 Corinthians 1:30–31
2 *Alive—1 Corinthians 15:22*
3 *Alive—Ephesians 2:4–7*
4 *Alive—Acts 17:24–28*
5 *Alive—John 1:1–4*
6 *Alive—Romans 6:10–13*
7 *Alive—1 John 4:9–12*

Week two:
8 *Alive—Romans 6:8–11*
9 *Alive—Colossians 2:13–15*
10 *Alive—John 6:57–58*
11 *Eternally alive—John 3:14–15*
12 *Eternally alive—John 3:16*
13 *Eternally alive—Romans 6:23*
14 *Eternally alive—John 4:13–14*

Week three:
15 *Eternally alive—John 6:40*
16 *Eternally alive—John 10:10*
17 *Eternally alive—1 John 5:12*
18 *Full of His life—Colossians 2:9–10*

In JESUS I am WEAK and LIVE by the power of GOD

On the Cross Jesus took upon Himself all the weaknesses of mankind—feebleness and disease of body and mind. Yet, now, through the abundant, mighty, miraculous power of God, Jesus is alive.

I, also, am feeble, diseased, and impotent, but I have been brought into His wholeness. The same force and strength God used to bring life out of death in Jesus have entered and are at work in me for His purpose, far exceeding what I could desire or imagine.

Father, as I burn physically with changes in my body, sometimes I am shocked by the passions of desire that rage in me.

April, Week one

Yet through this You enable me to be firm in my marriage commitment. The positive that comes out of my sinful nature when it is subdued by the Cross, is a deeper compassion for those who fall.

My child,

so many assume that they are only a composite of their failures and shortcomings. My passionate love is a searing laser that reaches through the physical and touches others. It reaches through your emotions, your dreams and longings, and through your most earnest intercessions in the Spirit.

Yes, I use you to love with My love, which is holy. It burns fiercely in you to cleanse you. It is My way to fight fire with fire.

"For indeed He was crucified because of weakness, yet He lives because of the power of God. For we also are weak in Him, yet we shall live with Him because of the power of God directed toward you."

2 Corinthians 13:4, NAS

In JESUS
I have LIFE

God's Word, His sure promise, His perfect
will, determination, desire, and pleasure
are life for those who receive Him. This
life in Christ Jesus is *theropia*, a wonderful
therapy! It has to do with healing—with
healthy creative relationships in the family.

In Him there is serving, care, and treat-
ment of the sick in such a way that
healing takes place.

Today was Susanna's First Communion. She has been a faithful, if
shy, student of mine in drawing,
colors, and embroidery. (She was
drawing the *malinche* flowers so I
put her in the border.) We walked
to Puerto Morazon. Rafael on his
crutches led the way over the
maze of boggy beach to the
sleepy fishing village.

April, Week two

Since there were no musicians prepared for the service, Rafael sang *De Colores* for Susanna. Now the priest, who only ventures there infrequently, knows we have a service each Sunday and has tasted of the joy we are experiencing as a "family." My cup runs over!

Father, I praise You for giving this life to me and pouring it through me to others.

My child,

wherever you are, there are those who will receive My Word through you as thirstily as an eager babe draws milk from its mother. Be centered in My place for you so that you are a relaxed, pure channel for that life-giving stream. Feed on My Word daily so that you will have fresh milk to give, healing to the bones.

"Paul, an apostle of Christ Jesus by the will of God according to the promise of the life which is in Christ Jesus, To Timothy, my beloved child: Grace, mercy, and peace from God the Father and Christ Jesus our Lord."

1 Timothy 2:1–2, RSV

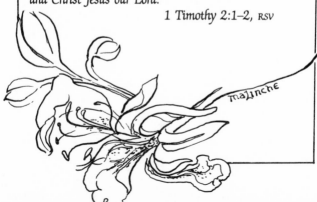

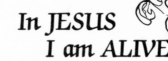

In JESUS
I am ALIVE

The death to self in baptism, in immersion into the Spirit of God in Jesus, releases in me the vital, eternal life of God. Just as surely as being human means that physical death will occur at some time, so being in Christ means I have supernatural life in Him through and beyond death.

Deaths are occurring around the world from governments that strangle the poor, that wipe out churches that would help the innocent. Yet here there seems to be an honest attempt to meet the needs of the poor and to encourage churches that have these same goals.

The Roman Empire in Jesus' day crushed the poor at will and brutally maintained power, but into that place You sent Your Son, unafraid of what men could do to Him, to die, yet to live again.

April, Week three

Father, how comforting to know that I can count on You in every circumstance in life and even through the unknown realm of death. I pray earnestly for those who do not have this confidence, and for those through whom death comes, for they do not see Jesus.

My child,

Paul saw the experience of death as planting a seed that would burst forth into a new form much more glorious than before.

Yes! Say *Yes!* to My life within you. Immersed in and filled with My Spirit of life, you will be cocooned, resting and yet pressing on, until you spring forth clothed in glory, like a butterfly.

"For as in Adam all die, so also in Christ all shall be made alive."

1 Corinthians 15:22, NAS

In JESUS I am ALIVE

Through union with Christ, though dead in sin, I have been made alive and joined with all others who believe in the Resurrection of Jesus. Now we are seated in heavenly places above the principalities and powers of darkness. We are to see the world and the nations from this spiritual perspective.

Father, it grieves me to see Christians fighting one another. We need to see Your ways more clearly, so that we can repent of our wicked ways!

I believe it was Agnes Sanford who showed me that an intercessor cannot take sides in wartime, but must earnestly desire Your love to permeate all peoples. Betsie ten Boom prayed as fervently

April, Week four

for the Nazis as Corrie prayed for those being hurt by them.

My child,

would you kill your own brother? Would you mutilate part of your own flesh? This is what is happening, for you have brothers and sisters in every nation. Preparing for war will never prevent evil. Only My Spirit will overcome the darkness. My way is always through the impossible, so that no man may glory.

''But God, being rich in mercy, because of His great love with which He loved us, even when we were dead in our transgressions, made us alive together with Christ . . . and raised us up with Him, and seated us with Him in the heavenly places.''

Ephesians 2:4–6, NAS

In *JESUS*

I

ABIDE

May

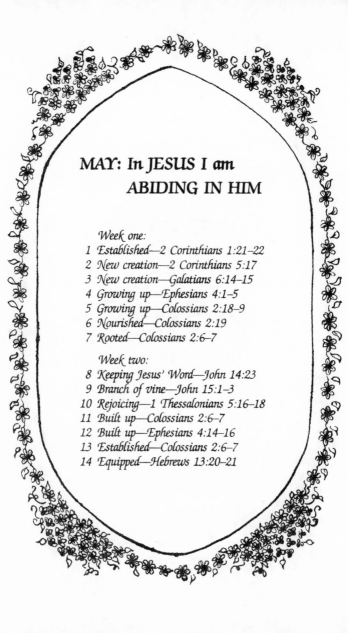

MAY: In JESUS I am
ABIDING IN HIM

Week one:
1 *Established—2 Corinthians 1:21–22*
2 *New creation—2 Corinthians 5:17*
3 *New creation—Galatians 6:14–15*
4 *Growing up—Ephesians 4:1–5*
5 *Growing up—Colossians 2:18–9*
6 *Nourished—Colossians 2:19*
7 *Rooted—Colossians 2:6–7*

Week two:
8 *Keeping Jesus' Word—John 14:23*
9 *Branch of vine—John 15:1–3*
10 *Rejoicing—1 Thessalonians 5:16–18*
11 *Built up—Colossians 2:6–7*
12 *Built up—Ephesians 4:14–16*
13 *Established—Colossians 2:6–7*
14 *Equipped—Hebrews 13:20–21*

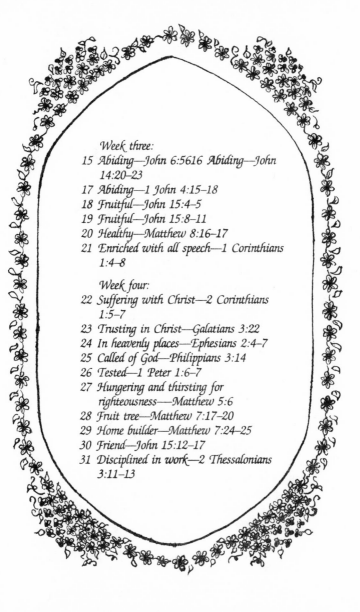

In JESUS
I am a
NEW CREATION

In freshness and newness of faith, I am a
Christian. Because God has done this, I am able
to follow in steps with Jesus, moving in an
orderly way within His boundaries, which
produces peace and mercy. This peace is oneness
with Him, quietness and rest, which results in
health and prosperity, and enables me to touch
others with His tenderness despite my faults.

Father, my weakness in this place has been a
frustration to me. Yet there are abilities You
have given me in communication, praise, and
cooking, which are affirmed as being important.
Julie cannot write letters, but is able to work
hard hours in the sun. Jim is devastated by the
heat, but has skills in group management,
working with machinery, and finding things.
These gifts are all indispensable for the project.

May, Week one

Each of us has wanted many times to quit,
feeling our specific contributions are so little.

My child,

the secret is in receiving who you are in Me.
Then, step by step, the wonderful plan I have for
your life is revealed. It is designed so that we
move together as one, knitted in a functional and
beautiful way with all others who know Me.
"See how they love one another!"

This is the effective, convincing witness.

"For neither is circumcision anything, nor
uncircumcision, but a new creation. And those
who will walk by this rule, peace and mercy be
upon them, and upon the Israel of God."
                                      Galatians 6:15–16, NAS

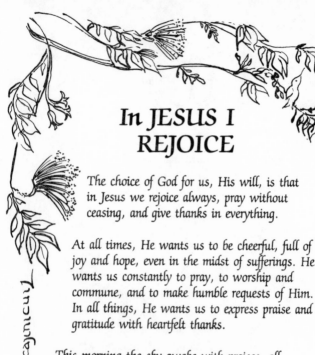

In JESUS I REJOICE

The choice of God for us, His will, is that in Jesus we rejoice always, pray without ceasing, and give thanks in everything.

At all times, He wants us to be cheerful, full of joy and hope, even in the midst of sufferings. He wants us constantly to pray, to worship and commune, and to make humble requests of Him. In all things, He wants us to express praise and gratitude with heartfelt thanks.

This morning the sky awoke with praises, all rosy and soft, but I only wanted to close my eyes and hide in the tent from another day.

I am tired of mosquitoes and flies, of soaking sweat. I am tired of innumerable eyes staring at me, speaking words I don't understand. So many are hungry for food I cannot give, wearing rags I cannot replace. Many are diseased without medicines, without hope for cure, unaware of Your healing power. Many call Your name, but do not expect You to act in their daily drudgery in a country torn by revolution.

May, Week two

I am angry that I am not God!

You have called us to break through walls of despair to see through Your eyes. Thank You for Rafael, Susanna, Magda, Celestino, Santiago, Pilar, Catalina . . . for so many who touch our lives, enriching us so that in giving we have received.

Yes, I can face today. Yes, I can praise You, the Prince of Peace.

My child,

the process is as important as the end product. The result of your anger is that you learn to trust and praise Me at a deeper level than if you had never needed to cry out. Expect Me to act as you draw near to hear the word that together we fulfill.

"Rejoice always; pray without ceasing; in everything give thanks; for this is God's will for you in Christ Jesus."

1 Thessalonians 5:16–18, NAS

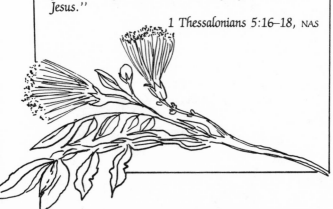

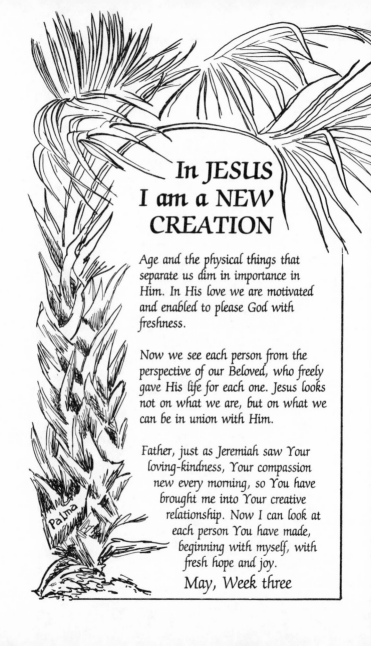

In JESUS I am a NEW CREATION

Age and the physical things that separate us dim in importance in Him. In His love we are motivated and enabled to please God with freshness.

Now we see each person from the perspective of our Beloved, who freely gave His life for each one. Jesus looks not on what we are, but on what we can be in union with Him.

Father, just as Jeremiah saw Your loving-kindness, Your compassion new every morning, so You have brought me into Your creative relationship. Now I can look at each person You have made, beginning with myself, with fresh hope and joy.

May, Week three

Yesterday Jim and I had our twenty-fifth wedding anniversary. Living with someone that long demands a lot of forgiveness and willingness to begin afresh.

At times each of us has felt the relationship impossible, but the Lord has given us new eyes of appreciation for each other, time and again. Sometimes that was from the heart and sometimes merely a decision of the will.

My child,

daily I am creating in you a clean heart, a renewed spirit. You will be prepared to be part of the new heavens and new earth in the new covenant that I have made with all who will leave behind what is dead, and enter into the joy of what I am doing now.

"Therefore if any man is in Christ, he is a new creature; the old things passed away; behold, new things have come."

2 Corinthians 5:17, NAS

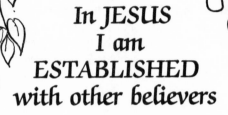

In JESUS
I am
ESTABLISHED
with other believers

Grefrut

God stabilizes us; He makes us secure and firm in our relationship with His Son, the Messiah, and with others who know Him. God Himself enables us to be faithful disciples.

This Hebrew concept is stated in Psalm 41:12: "Thou upholdest me in mine integrity, and settest me before thy face forever" (KJV). God grasps us securely. He holds us fast and sustains us. He is ever close.

Last week for the first time I climbed a hill laden with luscious tropical fruits to a high point overlooking Honduras, the Gulf of Fonseca, and El Salvador. What I saw was a blue-green jewel, sparkling and silent. I trembled to think of millions of dollars in military games so close.

May, Week four

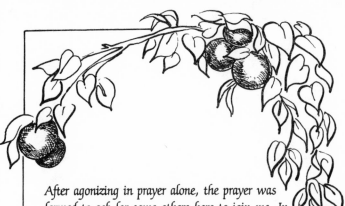

After agonizing in prayer alone, the prayer was formed to ask for some others here to join me. In this place of desperate need and armed conflict, God, I need to know Your heart to do spiritual warfare. Thank You for answering that prayer and sending my son Andy and others to join me.

My child,

I enable you to endure. Indeed, I need you so that in times of terror light will shine on the narrow path that leads—all who will come—home. You are not alone.

Remember you are My laborer in the harvest.

"Now He who establishes us with you in Christ and anointed us is God, who also sealed us and gave us the Spirit in our hearts as a pledge."
2 Corinthians 1:21–22, NAS

In JESUS
I am
FILLED
and
FREE

June

JUNE: In JESUS I am FILLED and FREE

Week one:

1 *Reconciled, at peace—Colossians 1:19–20*
2 *Reconciled, at peace—Romans 5:1–2*
3 *Reconciled, at peace—Romans 5:10–11*
4 *Reconciled, at peace—Philippians 4:6–7*
5 *Reconciled, at peace—John 16:33*
6 *Receptive of God's Spirit—Galatians 3:13–14*
7 *Receptive of God's Spirit—Hebrews 10:15–18*

Week two:

8 *Anointed—1 John 2:27*
9 *Filled with His Spirit—1 John 4:13*
10 *Sealed with Holy Spirit—Ephesians 1:13*
11 *Partaker of promise—Ephesians 3:4–7*
12 *Partaker of promise—2 Corinthians 1:20*
13 *Reconciled—2 Corinthians 5:18–20*
14 *Made innocent—Titus 3:4–7*

In JESUS I am made INNOCENT and PARTICIPATOR in all God has

Being made innocent, and free by His joyful liberality, benefiting from His pleasure in giving, I am a possessor and sharer in all He has.

Father, how little are those spools of thread, yet how precious to these people who have so little. To me they are tokens of the boxes of clothes we have ready to sell for just a tiny price so that the buyers have dignity and feel they are contributing to the project of building houses for those in need.

So many are in need. All but five houses in this community have dirt floors and roofs the rain pours through. There are only five refrigerators.

I dreamed one night that I had five refrigerators. A crowd of hungry people came in, but I sat in a corner eating some simple food, not knowing how to share my abundance.

June, Week one

I know Your Word is true for our physical needs as well as for our spiritual needs. O God, open wide the channel of thanksgiving here. Open the channels of giving in those who have so much they could share.

My child,

you know your weakness, your inability to meet the immensity of needs you see here. Yet, because you have tasted of My generosity toward you, you know it must be shared. So be it.

The more you give in My name, as I show you how, the more I give you to expand the circle of joy yet further. Overcoming the sting of poverty and death is My desire at work through you.

"The kindness and love of God our Saviour toward man appeared, not by works of righteousness which we have done, but according to his mercy he saved us, by the washing of regeneration, and renewing of the Holy Ghost; Which he shed on us abundantly through Jesus Christ our Saviour. . . ."

Titus 3:4–6, KJV

In JESUS I have the SPIRIT of LIFE

The holy breath of God in Jesus has moved in on the chaos of my existence and brought forth life, vital and vibrant. In Him death and discouragement must flee away for we have an indestructible fellowship of grace.

In the Hebrew, *chai* has an earthy sense: fresh green plants, running water. It also speaks of the congregation, the vigor of life within a community. Body, soul, and spirit are seen as a whole in the experience of life, the ability to exercise all one's energies to the fullest.

June, Week two

This morning Matthew played the tape recording of *Starry, Starry Night*, a folk ballad of the life of Vincent van Gogh. It is a haunting song that brings to mind the tragedy of the painter's life. Yet within the magnetism of this song is a strong death wish that must be resisted, and the line, "They never understood and perhaps they never will."

To be misunderstood is the risk any creative person must take. St. Francis countered self-pity by asking God's help in choosing to understand rather than to be understood.

Willingness on my part to reach out to others for healing has brought me to that solid ground of praise for *being*.

Father, quicken Your life within me. Well up within me those songs that speak the words on which You would have me focus. Penetrate my being with the abundant life that Jesus is.

My child,

I have made you and placed in you My seal of approval. Enjoy the life I have given you to the fullest. In union with Me, life is *good*.

"For the law of the Spirit of life in Christ has set you free from the law of sin and of death."

Romans 8:2, NAS

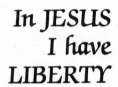

In JESUS I have LIBERTY

In the Messiah I have a relationship
that is free from arbitrary or despotic
control. In Him I have the freedom
to explore and enjoy the rights and
privileges given to me in His love.

Father, each of the independent church
groups here wants us to fit into its
rigid way of worship. They exclude
from Christianity all Catholics, and
anyone who drinks, smokes, or dances.

I appreciate much of what they are in You, but
these walls of exclusiveness and rejection of
others who deeply love You grieves me.

In North America the same is true. Members of
denominations cut themselves off from other
groups and nondenominational Christians believe
they have the only way.

June, Week three

I long to dance before You in the joyous moments of worship and praise, but the frowns of disapproval quench that desire.

My child,

there is a time to dance, and a time to refrain from dancing. As your pastor friend reminded you yesterday, the wheat and the weeds grow up together. It is not for you to pull up the others. Leave this harvest to the Lord.

Appreciate and participate in what you can with your brothers. Leave the rest with Me.

". . . I submitted to them the gospel which I preach among the Gentiles . . . because of the false brethren who had sneaked in to spy out our liberty which we have in Christ Jesus, in order to bring us into bondage."

Galatians 2:2–4, NAS

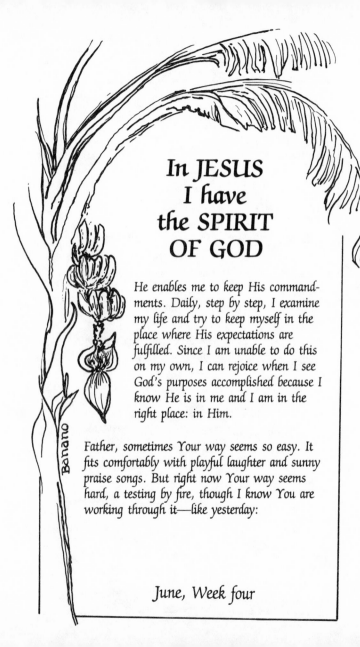

In JESUS
I have
the SPIRIT
OF GOD

He enables me to keep His commandments. Daily, step by step, I examine
my life and try to keep myself in the
place where His expectations are
fulfilled. Since I am unable to do this
on my own, I can rejoice when I see
God's purposes accomplished because I
know He is in me and I am in the
right place: in Him.

Father, sometimes Your way seems so easy. It
fits comfortably with playful laughter and sunny
praise songs. But right now Your way seems
hard, a testing by fire, though I know You are
working through it—like yesterday:

Banana

June, Week four

First, talking with Rafael, I revealed my sinfulness. Though this process of honesty is painful, it is a gift from Your Holy Spirit to enable me to live in the clear light without illusions of any holiness apart from Your mercy to me. I know the fires within are being carefully tended by Your Spirit to remove every impurity.

Then in the middle of the night, men drunk from the Saturday night fiesta emptied their rifle clips rapid fire just a few yards from where Jim, Matthew, and I lay sleeping in the tent.

I just had to sigh, "Thank You, Lord, for Your cleansing. Thank You that I am in the place where You have me, that I am ready to live or to die."

My child,

death to self through honesty sets you free from fear of man and of physical death. Think of the brilliant rainbow of colors arching over the flood waters, and imagine what glory is revealed when you pass through fire. Truly the Son of Man is with you in the flames.

"And the one who keeps His commandments abides in Him, and He in him. And we know by this that He abides in us, by the Spirit which He has given us."

1 John 3:24, NAS

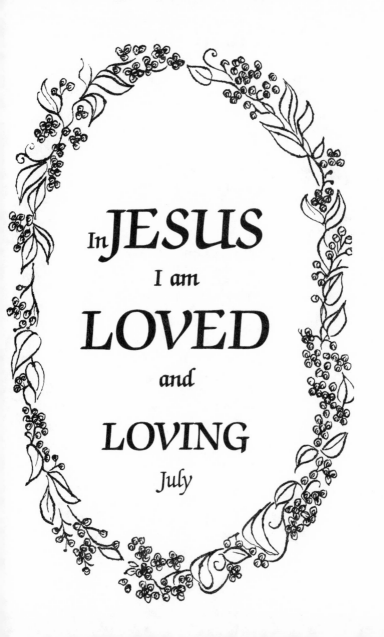

In **JESUS**
I am
LOVED
and
LOVING
July

JULY: In JESUS I am LOVED and LOVING

Week one:
1 *Saved for His purpose*—2 Timothy 1:7–9
2 *Strong in grace*—2 Timothy 2:1–2
3 *Blessed*—Ephesians 1:3–6
4 *Standing in grace*—Romans 5:1–2
5 *Faithful through love*—Galatians 5:5–6
6 *Faithful through love*—1 Timothy 1:12–16
7 *Faithful through love*—2 Timothy 1:13–14

Week two:
8 *Blessed*—Galatians 3:13–14
9 *Blessed*—Galatians 1:3–5
10 *Walking in love*—1 John 2:4–6
11 *Walking in love*—1 John 2:8–10
12 *Walking in love*—1 John 3:14
13 *Forgiven*—Ephesians 1:7–12
14 *Forgiven*—Colossians 1:13–14

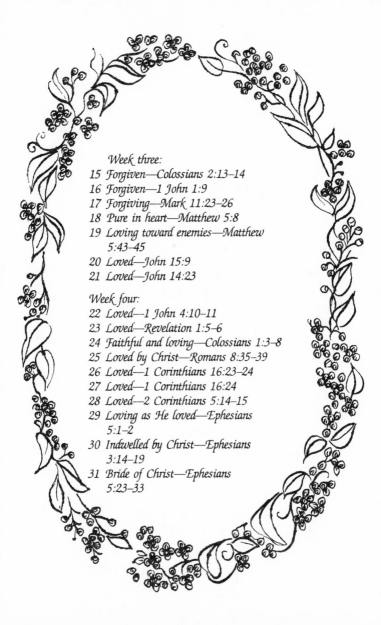

In JESUS I have GRACE, FAITH, and LOVE in abundance

Though I have in myself nothing but sinfulness and separation, Jesus has broken through with help. This gift is liberally given and fills my heart with divine joy and thanksgiving.

One night this week, after a joyful service with Catholic charismatics, we visited Doña Santos in El Viejo. There we were served a lightly fermented refresca. Though even the children were not affected, I had a dangerous "toxic chemical reaction." With no self-control, I shouted, laughed, and cried, and was unable to walk alone.

The next day, Jim helped me see how my frustrations had been revealed in my volatile actions. I was angry at not being able to control my environment here.

July, Week one

My head swirled for two days with wild thoughts, but I could tell when the deep, deep love of Jesus penetrated with peace and joy.

Father, thank You for speaking to my heart words of Scripture and songs of praise when my mind was not functioning. Thank You for exposing the roots of my anger, and for my being able to share openly with Jim.

My child,

I am patient with you. Be assured that I set you free from the world's grip so that you can respond to My gifts and share them.

"And the grace of our Lord was more than abundant . . . . Christ Jesus came into the world to save sinners, among whom I am foremost of all. And yet for this reason I found mercy. . . ."
1 Timothy 1:14–16, NAS

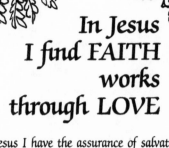

In Jesus
I find FAITH
works
through LOVE

In Jesus I have the assurance of salvation
and of His fidelity, which enables me to be
faithful and reliant on His love. That
conviction expresses itself first through His
unselfish *agape* love for me. Then I return
devotion to Him, and feel concern for the
good of others, which goes beyond legalism.

A statement of Gandhi's struck me as
true. He decided, from reading about Jesus
in the Gospels, that every means must be
consistent with the end, and that this
applies to nations as well as individuals.

In the same Spirit of Jesus, I must relate
to others, individuals and nations, all the
while examining myself, lest in my
''rightness'' I miss the mark.

July, Week two

Father, please show me self-righteousness and legalism in my life that crowd out the delight in my love for You.

When my heart strays from that singleness of love for You, then those around me miss out on the special way You give them love through me.

My child,

My hand is extended to you to turn your mourning into dancing. My arms are around you. Let Me lead. Keep your eyes on Me. As I embrace you, I give you all you need for each moment, teaching you the steps as we move together as one.

"For we through the Spirit, by faith, are waiting for the hope of righteousness. For in Christ Jesus neither circumcision nor uncircumcision means anything, but faith working through love."
Galatians 5:5–6, NAS

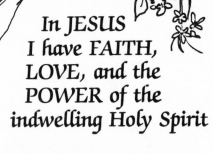

Sacuanjoche - Flor nacional

In JESUS I have FAITH, LOVE, and the POWER of the indwelling Holy Spirit

This enables me to walk in the way of truth. I must hold fast to the standard, the living Word of Jesus, for He gives me the ability to be true to the pattern He has shown. He loves me, and enables me to participate in a feast of love as I learn to pour out affection on friends and enemies alike.

I was dismayed the other day to read a letter from a precious Christian sister. She questioned our work here, wondering about the political stance of the poor people we are helping. She asked whether or not we realize we may be serving the enemy.

July, Week three

Our experience here has been so different from the tone of these questions. Every day little children in rags come on their way to school. I sharpen pencils for them and give them drinks of water. Are they the enemy?

Every day young men and old work long hours in the sun building houses. One of these, Feliz, a Sandinista, wants us to start a daily prayer time for workers. Is he the enemy?

Even if he is the enemy, what does Jesus say about my relationship to him?

My child,

as you see Me in the poor, you will learn of Me. As you serve Me in your enemy, you will become like Me. Soak yourself daily in My Word and listen for My inner voice of direction. This will enable you to walk steadily in My ways. My love makes you an overcomer.

"Retain the standard of sound words which you have heard . . . . Guard through the Holy Spirit who dwells in us, the treasure which has been entrusted to you."

2 Timothy 1:13–14, NAS

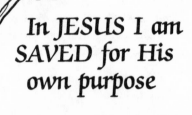

In JESUS I am SAVED for His own purpose

The miraculous strength of God enables us to suffer hardships with other believers in order to share God's good news. As the shrewbread in the Temple was spread before Him according to God's intention, so our lives are set before Him, exposed and used as He wills.

The believers here are a constant inspiration to me. One dentist in Managua, with an infectious grin, remarked that every day here is an adventure proving the faithful provisions of God. He leaned over and whispered to me, "There is no one good except Jesus."

In a way, that is comforting. Though we know God has called us here, still so often my humanness gets in the way of a holy example. But then, the people see me humbled and in need of

July, Week four

forgiveness and can believe this same forgiveness is for them.

Father, even though I don't like the hardships and the pressures here, I must rest in Your Word that it is for my own good. You will bring me through. You will help the needy ones.

My child,

My purpose is clear. There is salvation for individuals who seek Me and healing for nations who bow only to Me. I wipe away every tear and touch every hurt with compassion. Where you are weak, I come to you in brothers and sisters. I enable you to endure through it all.

"For God has not given us a spirit of timidity, but of power and love and discipline. Therefore . . . join with me in suffering for the gospel according to the power of God . . . ."

2 Timothy 1:7–9, NAS

In JESUS
I am
CLEANSED

August

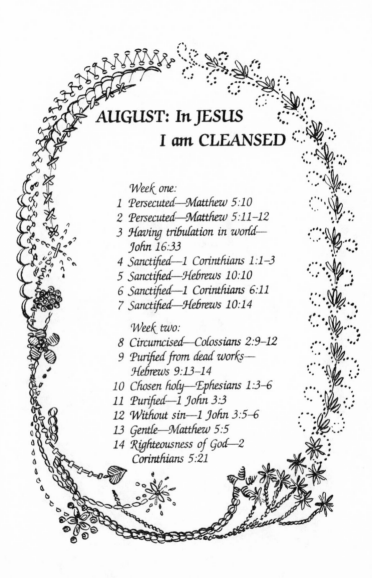

AUGUST: In JESUS I am CLEANSED

Week one:
1 *Persecuted—Matthew 5:10*
2 *Persecuted—Matthew 5:11–12*
3 *Having tribulation in world—*
   John 16:33
4 *Sanctified—1 Corinthians 1:1–3*
5 *Sanctified—Hebrews 10:10*
6 *Sanctified—1 Corinthians 6:11*
7 *Sanctified—Hebrews 10:14*

Week two:
8 *Circumcised—Colossians 2:9–12*
9 *Purified from dead works—*
   Hebrews 9:13–14
10 *Chosen holy—Ephesians 1:3–6*
11 *Purified—1 John 3:3*
12 *Without sin—1 John 3:5–6*
13 *Gentle—Matthew 5:5*
14 *Righteousness of God—2*
   Corinthians 5:21

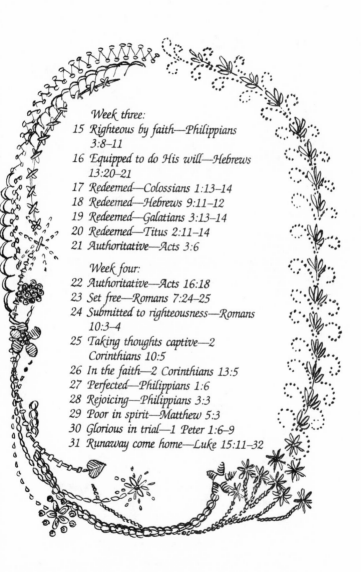

In JESUS I am SANCTIFIED

I am made *kadash*: holy, purified, and conse-
crated for God's use. That word was used for
those taking the Nazarite vows. Now every
believer, through the Messiah, belongs to the
sphere of the sacred, and is kosher, or clean
before God.

Father, how awesome to realize what You have
done. Me? *Holy*? How can I believe this? Yet,
because You see me this way, You enable me to
see myself and others as holy, too.

Saturday Rafael typed up a joke license to ''look
for women in all of Nicaragua.'' Immediately
Matthew and Daniel wanted to make one too.

It made me angry to see how easily they viewed
women as sex objects. So I made them a license
in my best calligraphy: ''To look for daughters of
God in all Nicaragua.'' In order to do this, the

August, Week one

license read, "you must see them as holy and pure in the eyes of God." We talked about Don Quixote and how his seeing the prostitute as a fine lady helped her become that.

I am thankful that Rafael readily accepted my "license" and led Matthew in burning the others.

My child,

when you truly grasp the significance of your holiness, your joy will overflow, for you will know the wonder of intimacy with your God. What I have called clean, let no one call dirty, inadequate, or unworthy.

". . . To those who have been sanctified in Christ Jesus, saints by calling, with all who in every place call upon the name of our Lord Jesus Christ . . ."

1 Corinthians 1:2, NAS

In JESUS I am HEALED by His wounds

When I endure suffering through no fault of my own, this is a gift pleasing to God. In this I follow in the tracks of Jesus. When people shouted at Him, Jesus did not answer in anger. When He experienced pain, He did not threaten those hurting Him. He surrendered the judgment to His Father, whose decisions are fair and right.

In His body He took all our sins so that we, being dead to sins, could live the way He lived. We were made whole by the blows that bruised Him.

Father, still weak from yesterday's sickness, I sit in the *casita* and can hear bombs in the distance. To this same *casita* every Sunday come the people of German Pomares—young and old, rich and poor, male and female, North American and Central American—with problems, sicknesses. Over and over again we have prayed, rejoicing in

August, Week two

Limón

Your healing act on the Cross. We have seen You work quietly and steadily to answer every prayer. You are building faith into us all, and the humility to ask expectantly, thankfully. Still we hear the bombs.

My child,

all the resources I give you are to be poured into living as I lived. My life in you is the same as the Life that gave itself and brought forth healing.

"If when you do what is right and suffer for it you patiently endure it, this finds favor with God. For you have been called for this purpose, sinced Christ also suffered for you, leaving you an example for you to follow in His steps, who committed no sin, nor was any deceit found in His mouth . . . and He Himself bore our sins in His body on the cross, that we might die to sin and live to righteousness; for by His wounds you were healed."

1 Peter 2:20–24, NAS

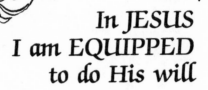

In JESUS
I am EQUIPPED
to do His will

pascua

In other words, through the channel of Jesus, we
are thoroughly fit, and joined together in the
good efforts, occupations, labors He gives us to do.

Father, such distressing, large forces are at work,
even among those who are called Christians.
Opposite points of view and approaches cause
stubborn declarations. Bullets are even aimed at
brothers and sisters.

This should not be, yet I sense the same struggl-
ings wrestling inside me.

That lifestyle of Jesus, that peace in which He
walked through the political and religious and
social dichotomies of His day, is what I must
use as a polestar. He will guide me to that
unifying place of Your peace in the midst of
warrings in the world. Help!

August, Week three

My child,

I know what is in man. Understand that it is deceptive to believe that by building better bombs a nation brings about My peace. It is a lie to believe that to kill the enemy protects the innocent.

Love does not kill human enemies. When the United States, Russia, Nicaragua, or any other nation depends on armaments instead of on Me, you can be sure armaments will be needed, for violence breeds violence.

The way of peace is the only way, the only reality, the only security, the only purity that does not violate anyone. It gives itself again and again and again . . . .

"[May God] equip you with everything good that you may do his will, working in you that which is pleasing in his sight . . . ."

Hebrews 13:21, RSV

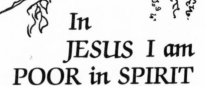

In
JESUS I am
POOR in SPIRIT

In Jesus I am blessed to have my poverty of
spirit, my total inadequacy to perform God's will
on my own, exposed publicly.

Utterly dependent on Him for daily necessities, I
come to His throne room, aware of the filthy
rags of my own good works. I cringe as a pauper
before the King of the universe.

And I am filled to overflowing with His generosity; I am supremely blessed.

Father, Luke's Gospel does not qualify the
statement of Jesus. He simply says, "Blessed are
the poor." As I am in touch with the poor here,
I see two kinds of poverty: those despairing or
hardened by their need, and those who continue

August, Week four

to seek You and are thankful and generous in the midst of desperate circumstances.

Jesus also said it is more difficult to be rich in this world than to be poor. How hard this is to understand.

My child,

Job's friends sat before his poverty in silence for seven days. Even then their advice was wrong.

An angry heart rebukes Me for allowing wretchedness in the world. A pliable, teachable heart recognizes Me in the poor. And if you have two of anything, you are free to give. In this the very nature of My reign in the heavenlies is revealed.

"Blessed are the poor in spirit, for theirs is the kingdom of heaven."

Matthew 5:3, NAS

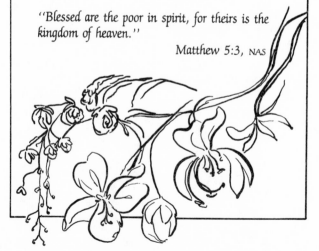

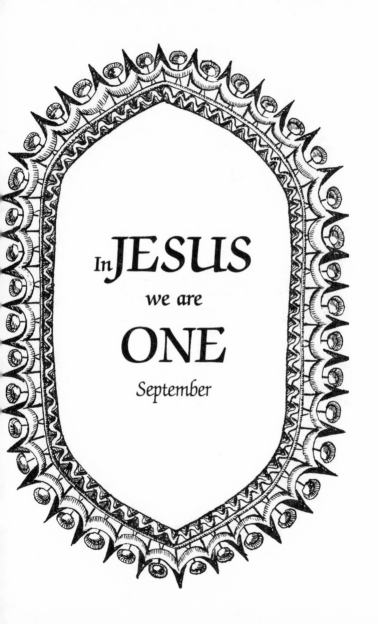

In JESUS
we are
ONE
September

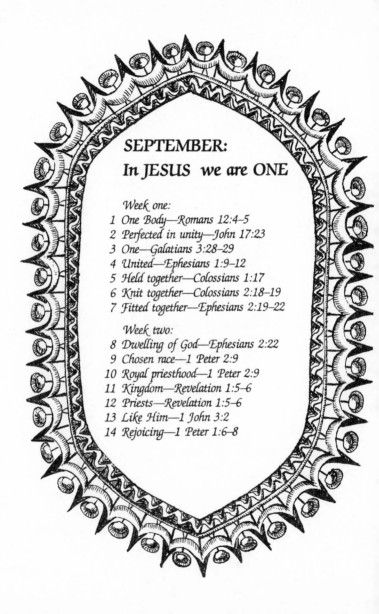

SEPTEMBER:
In JESUS we are ONE

Week one:
1 One Body—Romans 12:4–5
2 Perfected in unity—John 17:23
3 One—Galatians 3:28–29
4 United—Ephesians 1:9–12
5 Held together—Colossians 1:17
6 Knit together—Colossians 2:18–19
7 Fitted together—Ephesians 2:19–22

Week two:
8 Dwelling of God—Ephesians 2:22
9 Chosen race—1 Peter 2:9
10 Royal priesthood—1 Peter 2:9
11 Kingdom—Revelation 1:5–6
12 Priests—Revelation 1:5–6
13 Like Him—1 John 3:2
14 Rejoicing—1 Peter 1:6–8

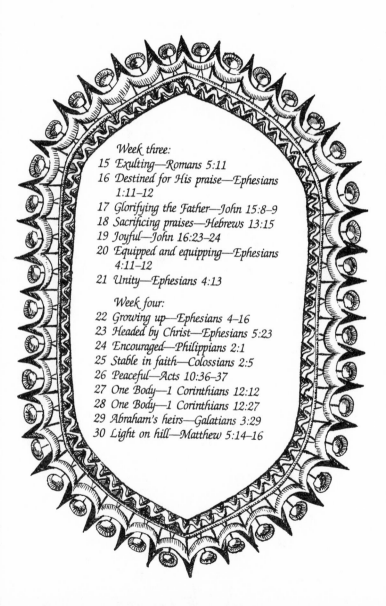

In JESUS we are ONE with all who have believed

Together we reflect and add to His splendor.

At the right time the Messiah will gather together all those who have loved Him. The Jewish Christians who first hoped in Him, and those of the Old Covenant who trusted in the promised Messiah, will join with us who believe on Him without seeing Him. Together, as one, we will glow with the brightness of giving to God the worship and praise due Him.

It has been a joy to visit and worship with a rich variety of Christians all over Nicaragua, to feel we are a link, a bridge between these and our own varieties of believers in the United States.

September, Week one

My Father, what a joy to participate now in the reaching and stretching of my being, joining with all others throughout history who praise and glorify You. You are worthy!

My child,

as you enter into the realms of praise, all things take on the characteristics of My Kingdom. In a small way the veil is lifted and you begin to see My perspective. Test your perspective with My Word. Is it good news to the poor?

". . . We have obtained an inheritance . . . to the end that we who were the first to hope in Christ should be to the praise of His glory. In Him, you also, after listening to the message of truth, the gospel of your salvation—having also believed, you were sealed in Him with the Holy Spirit of promise . . . ."

Ephesians 1:11–13, NAS

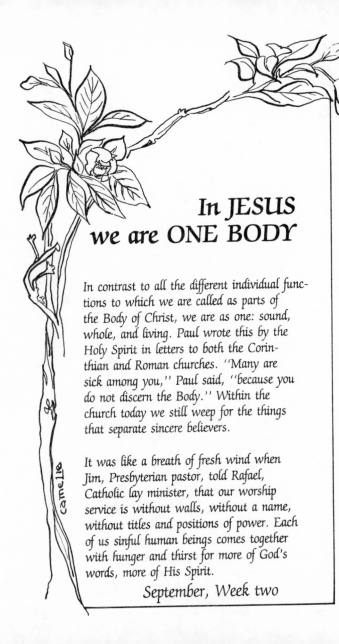

In JESUS
we are ONE BODY

In contrast to all the different individual functions to which we are called as parts of
the Body of Christ, we are as one: sound,
whole, and living. Paul wrote this by the
Holy Spirit in letters to both the Corin-
thian and Roman churches. "Many are
sick among you," Paul said, "because you
do not discern the Body." Within the
church today we still weep for the things
that separate sincere believers.

It was like a breath of fresh wind when
Jim, Presbyterian pastor, told Rafael,
Catholic lay minister, that our worship
service is without walls, without a name,
without titles and positions of power. Each
of us sinful human beings comes together
with hunger and thirst for more of God's
words, more of His Spirit.

September, Week two

Father, please give us eyes to see the value of each one called by Your name. In our efforts to be "right," even as the Pharisees, let us not find ourselves wielding axes to amputate parts of Your Body that we need to do Your will.

My child,

only I can knit together such strong and willful parts. Let My Holy Spirit move in you freely to break down walls of separation and to build up appreciation of the gifts I have given others.

"For just as in a single human body there are many limbs and organs, all with different functions, so all of us, united with Christ, form one body, serving individually as limbs and organs to one another."

Romans 12:4–5, NEB

In JESUS I am ONE with all other believers

In Him our differences are utilized fully. We are in a spiritual sense "married" to all other believers, even as husband and wife are one flesh.

Father, I have seen so many "rugged individualists" in the Christian life. They seem to be conspicuous targets for the evil one. It is often easier to "do my own thing" than to flow and agree with my brothers and sisters in You.

What a lesson I have learned from watching our son James play the contra bass in the Asheville, North Carolina, Symphony. He has long amazed me at his willingness to pour his musical talents into essentially a background instrument. Rarely does the bass player have a solo part. Yet how rich and full that deep resonant sound makes the symphony.

September, Week three

I like to think that when Jesus conducts this life's symphony, our instruments will fit in with the others and contribute to the overall beauty intended by the Author of all music.

My child,

as you learn to yield to those who love Me, you will see the true measure of how you yield to Me.

''There is neither Jew nor Greek, there is neither bond nor free, there is neither male nor female: for ye are all one in Christ Jesus. And if ye be Christ's then are ye Abraham's seed, and heirs according to the promise.''

Galatians 3:28–29, KJV

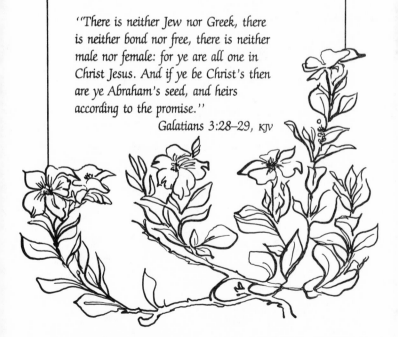

In JESUS
we are ONE

We are Abraham's children, heirs in the family of God.

In Him the distinctions that separate and divide people have no value in measuring who we are. The precious seed of God's life has been planted in us.

When Christina and Rafael took Matthew and me to the Nicaraguense Campesino Music Festival, I had a big surprise. Many in the audience were Russians, yet they looked exactly like our North American friends. There were young women who looked like school teachers, and older men who could have been university professors.

"Equales," Christina and Rafael both said. ''People from Russia and the U.S. are just alike to us.''

September, Week four

This bothered me for a week until one prayer meeting in the grass hut of Pastor Francisco Jiminez. After praying on our knees on the dirt floor, he said, "Lord Jesus is preparing a place where there is no suffering and pain. We must never give up the struggle to walk in His holy way. You have a lot of things, but what you have isn't important. God sees the heart. In Him we are equals."

My child,

it takes time for seeds to feel secure enough in new ground to stretch forth tendrils of hope that something so good is truly theirs. You have been planted in this ground awhile; it is important for you to tend the newly sown. Encourage them to bask in My sun, drink in My rain until they are freed from the hard shell of prejudice binding them and can burst forth with joy into My family.

". . . For ye are all one in Christ Jesus. And if ye be Christ's, then are ye Abraham's seed, and heirs according to the promise."

Galatians 3:28–29, KJV

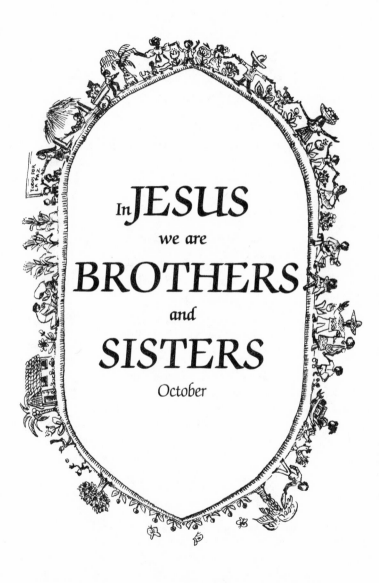

In JESUS
we are
BROTHERS
and
SISTERS
October

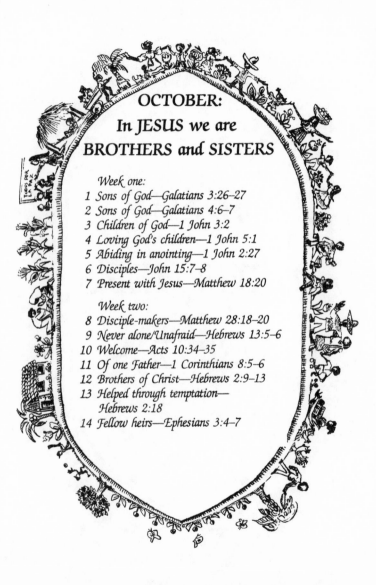

OCTOBER:

In JESUS we are

BROTHERS and SISTERS

Week one:
1 *Sons of God—Galatians 3:26–27*
2 *Sons of God—Galatians 4:6–7*
3 *Children of God—1 John 3:2*
4 *Loving God's children—1 John 5:1*
5 *Abiding in anointing—1 John 2:27*
6 *Disciples—John 15:7–8*
7 *Present with Jesus—Matthew 18:20*

Week two:
8 *Disciple-makers—Matthew 28:18–20*
9 *Never alone/Unafraid—Hebrews 13:5–6*
10 *Welcome—Acts 10:34–35*
11 *Of one Father—1 Corinthians 8:5–6*
12 *Brothers of Christ—Hebrews 2:9–13*
13 *Helped through temptation—*
   Hebrews 2:18
14 *Fellow heirs—Ephesians 3:4–7*

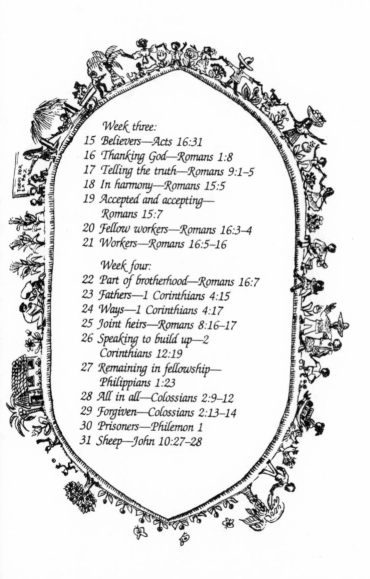

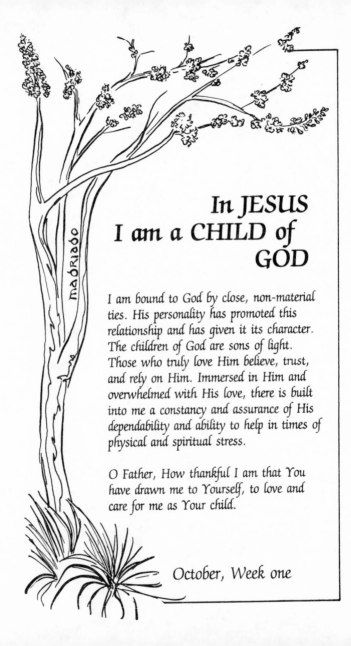

In JESUS
I am a CHILD of
GOD

I am bound to God by close, non-material
ties. His personality has promoted this
relationship and has given it its character.
The children of God are sons of light.
Those who truly love Him believe, trust,
and rely on Him. Immersed in Him and
overwhelmed with His love, there is built
into me a constancy and assurance of His
dependability and ability to help in times of
physical and spiritual stress.

O Father, How thankful I am that You
have drawn me to Yourself, to love and
care for me as Your child.

October, Week one

Father, I want to see more clearly who You are, what You are doing, and to know Your ways, Your thoughts.

My child,

how it pleases Me to have children who want to grow, to stretch beyond the comfort of warm blankets and milk, who are willing to be like My firstborn, Jesus. Jesus gave Me His will. In that giving is both death and resurrection.

"For ye are all the children of God by faith in Christ Jesus. For as many of you as have been baptized into Christ have put on Christ."

Galatians 3:26–27, KJV

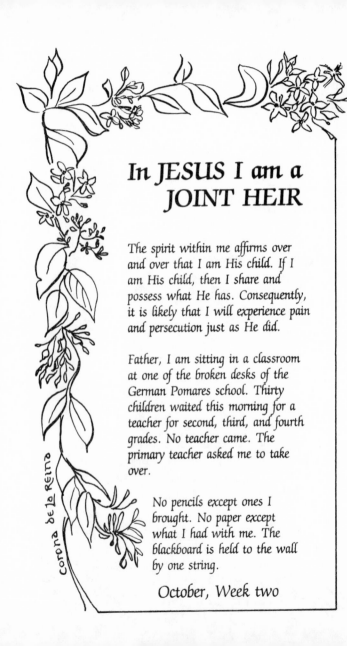

In JESUS I am a JOINT HEIR

The spirit within me affirms over and over that I am His child. If I am His child, then I share and possess what He has. Consequently, it is likely that I will experience pain and persecution just as He did.

Father, I am sitting in a classroom at one of the broken desks of the German Pomares school. Thirty children waited this morning for a teacher for second, third, and fourth grades. No teacher came. The primary teacher asked me to take over.

No pencils except ones I brought. No paper except what I had with me. The blackboard is held to the wall by one string.

October, Week two

corona de la Reina

I had wondered before we came
what the attitude would be here.
The things I had feared have been
shadow tigers. The need here is so
great there is only gratitude for
whoever would help. The suffering I
experience here is not persecution for
my faith, but a wrenching of body,
soul, and spirit at the poverty of
these children. They hold up empty
cups ready to receive whatever is
given. O Lord, let us give them
Your love. Let them know in You
their uniqueness and possibilities.

My child,

often the suffering you expect is only
a fear that is of man's making. Love
passes through the fears and meets
Me in the needs.

"The Spirit Himself bears witness
with our spirit that we are children
of God, and if children, heirs also,
heirs of God and fellow heirs with
Christ, if indeed we suffer with Him
in order that we may also be
           glorified with Him."
                    Romans 8:16–17, NAS

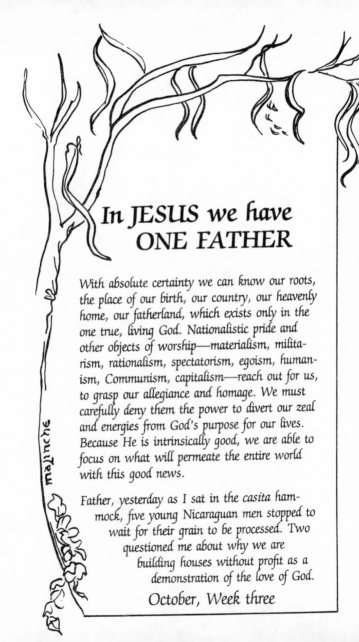

In JESUS we have ONE FATHER

With absolute certainty we can know our roots, the place of our birth, our country, our heavenly home, our fatherland, which exists only in the one true, living God. Nationalistic pride and other objects of worship—materialism, militarism, rationalism, spectatorism, egoism, humanism, Communism, capitalism—reach out for us, to grasp our allegiance and homage. We must carefully deny them the power to divert our zeal and energies from God's purpose for our lives. Because He is intrinsically good, we are able to focus on what will permeate the entire world with this good news.

Father, yesterday as I sat in the *casita* hammock, five young Nicaraguan men stopped to wait for their grain to be processed. Two questioned me about why we are building houses without profit as a demonstration of the love of God.

October, Week three

malinche

Then they wanted to see our photograph album, which brought questions that were difficult to answer: How can the people of such a nation of wealth as the U.S.A. not show brotherly love to Nicaraguans, or to refugees, or to the poor?

"Isn't the U.S.A. made up of people from other countries?" one asked.

My child,

Lazarus will always sit at the door making the rich man uncomfortable. The response is crucial, for individuals and for nations. To hoard is hell, to share is divine. You see those here with so little freely giving what they have. You are also worn out with the begging of others. Trust that My provision for you is as powerful as My compassion moving through you to those in need.

"For though there be that are called gods, whether in heaven or in earth, (as there be gods many, and lords many). But to us there is but one God, the Father, of whom are all things, and we in him; and one Lord Jesus Christ, by whom are all things, and we by him."

1 Corinthians 8:5–6, KJV

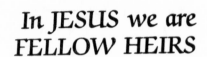

In JESUS we are FELLOW HEIRS

We are of the same Body, and partakers of His promise. Together we receive all that God has. As fellow members of the Christian community, we belong to the same body. As co-participants in Him, we share with believers in His outpoured Holy Spirit.

Father, You have given me so much that often I feel glutted. But give me one thing more: the grace you gave Paul to be a servant-minister, *diakonos*—one who runs Your errands, waits on Your table, and does whatever menial duties You need to have done. One who is faithful.

October, Week four

My child,

that gift is the most precious one I have, for it enables you to be more like Me, like the Messiah you love. To be a servant is to recognize your own need, your poverty, which looks to Me for everything. To be a servant is to consider others better than yourself, with joy recognizing their strengths.

You can also look with wonder and pleasure on the robes and rings and fiestas I bestow on you just because I love and forgive you.

To please Me is your highest goal, so no hardship is too great. I give you My Spirit to enable you to complete the task.

". . . Understand my insight into the mystery of Christ . . . to be specific, that the Gentiles are fellow heirs and fellow members of the body, and fellow partakers of the promise in Christ Jesus through the gospel, of which I was made a minister, according to the gift of God's grace which was given to me according to the working of His power."

Ephesians 3:4–7, NAS

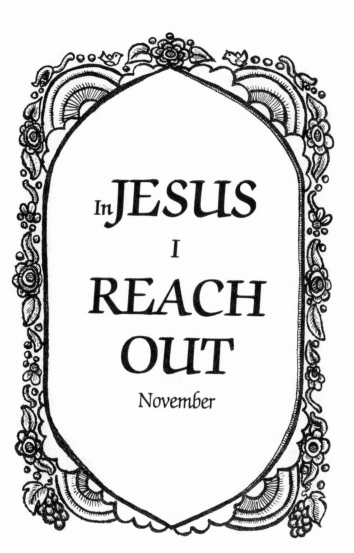

In JESUS
I
REACH
OUT

November

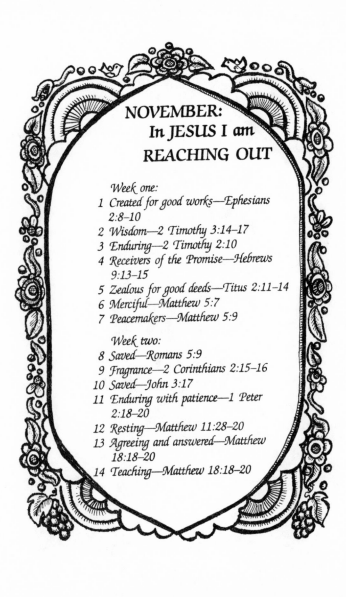

NOVEMBER:
In JESUS I am
REACHING OUT

Week one:
1 *Created for good works—Ephesians 2:8–10*
2 *Wisdom—2 Timothy 3:14–17*
3 *Enduring—2 Timothy 2:10*
4 *Receivers of the Promise—Hebrews 9:13–15*
5 *Zealous for good deeds—Titus 2:11–14*
6 *Merciful—Matthew 5:7*
7 *Peacemakers—Matthew 5:9*

Week two:
8 *Saved—Romans 5:9*
9 *Fragrance—2 Corinthians 2:15–16*
10 *Saved—John 3:17*
11 *Enduring with patience—1 Peter 2:18–20*
12 *Resting—Matthew 11:28–20*
13 *Agreeing and answered—Matthew 18:18–20*
14 *Teaching—Matthew 18:18–20*

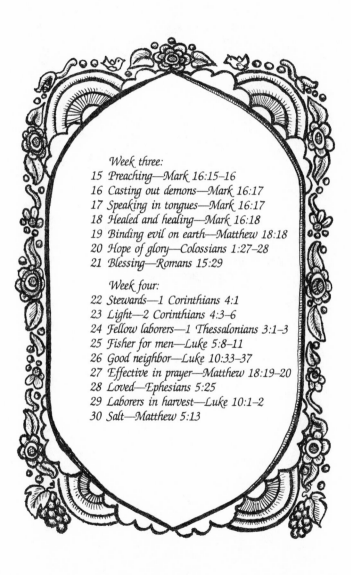

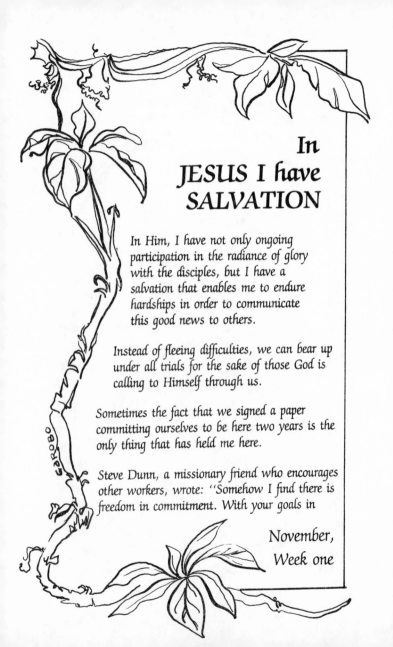

In
JESUS I have
SALVATION

In Him, I have not only ongoing
participation in the radiance of glory
with the disciples, but I have a
salvation that enables me to endure
hardships in order to communicate
this good news to others.

Instead of fleeing difficulties, we can bear up
under all trials for the sake of those God is
calling to Himself through us.

Sometimes the fact that we signed a paper
committing ourselves to be here two years is the
only thing that has held me here.

Steve Dunn, a missionary friend who encourages
other workers, wrote: "Somehow I find there is
freedom in commitment. With your goals in

November,
Week one

focus you are free to invest your time and energy, and even your very lives, to see them come to pass. You are free to serve the Lord with all your heart, with all your mind, with all your soul, and with all your strength.''

O God, in order to fulfill this great task, I must stay close to You to discern, to hear Your voice, to feel the pressure of Your hand nudging me to spend time and energy in prayer and acts of love for certain ones in my sphere of influence. As I appreciate what You have done for me more, I will be able to endure more in order that others may rejoice in Your love for them.

My child,

My plan is perfect. By being willing to extend yourself to others to draw them to Me, you will find that My strength floods through your weakness and inability. You will have all you need to do the hard thing, and indeed, will see the beauty I have built into it. There is no greater work than drawing a little one to know Me.

''Therefore I endure everything for the sake of the elect, that they also may obtain the salvation which in Christ Jesus goes with eternal glory.''

2 Timothy 2:10, RSV

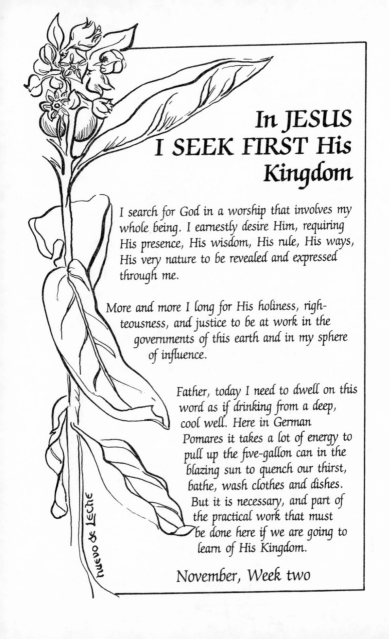

In JESUS I SEEK FIRST His Kingdom

I search for God in a worship that involves my whole being. I earnestly desire Him, requiring His presence, His wisdom, His rule, His ways, His very nature to be revealed and expressed through me.

More and more I long for His holiness, righteousness, and justice to be at work in the governments of this earth and in my sphere of influence.

Father, today I need to dwell on this word as if drinking from a deep, cool well. Here in German Pomares it takes a lot of energy to pull up the five-gallon can in the blazing sun to quench our thirst, bathe, wash clothes and dishes. But it is necessary, and part of the practical work that must be done here if we are going to learn of His Kingdom.

November, Week two

nuevo de leche

Yesterday I was saddened to learn some of the Christians here meet every day from six A.M. to noon and often all night. Is this seeking first God's Kingdom when they could be offering their families practical help from the wretched sickness and poverty? When their children are dying from dysentery?

Father, help me know how best to reflect Your Kingdom.

My child,

it is not for you to judge the spirituality of others, but to hold My Word like a flame to illumine the darkness of your spirit.

Once you have seen how My Gospel is *good news* to the poor and enables the rich to become cheerful givers, and how all are participants in My government, your sadness will be penetrated with joy.

"Do not be anxious then, saying, 'What shall we eat?' or 'What shall we drink?' . . . For your heavenly Father knows that you need all these things. But seek first His kingdom . . . and all these things shall be added to you."

Matthew 6:31–33, NAS

In JESUS
we are His
WORKMANSHIP

God has healed and preserved us, given us salvation, and made us whole by a sacrificial gift. It is not by our own strength or efforts, lest we should have pride in ourselves.

God has made us what we are. In His plans there are prepared beforehand certain good deeds that will flow forth from us as we are responsive to Him.

Father, I don't want to be caught up in dead works—good things You have not directed me to do. Joni has a song that Matthew and I play often: "I am willing, Lord . . . to be just exactly what You want me to be." She asks to be content to do only those things God has designed for her.

Many times it is hard for me to be satisfied with only that. False guilt enters in and I feel I

November, Week three

Flor de San Pablo

should be out there sweating at the project, counting of less value the tasks I have to do here at our *granero* home like having meals ready on time.

My child,

as you yield to Me, you will find the things you are required to do to be less, yet more effective. You will find a rhythm of living that flows with My Spirit through your body, soul, and spirit. It is unique to you, yet identifiable as authentic witness, linking and merging with other believers, reaching and touching the poor with good news, the captives with freedom, the sick with healing, the lonely with meaningful relationships.

"For by grace are ye saved through faith: and that not of yourselves; it is the gift of God: Not of works lest any man should boast. For we are his workmanship, created in Christ Jesus for good works, which God hath before ordained that we should walk in them."

Ephesians 2:8–10, KJV

In JESUS
I have HOPE of
GLORY

This hope of glory flows through me to others. We must gently teach every person the way to become complete, mature in Jesus.

Father, in order to care that much about others, in order to have the persistence and commitment not to give up on anyone and not to lose heart myself, I need You in me more. The hope of glory, my expectation, needs to be based in the consistent awareness of Your glorious Presence, which fills me with praise.

It has been a joy to see the unfolding of Your will in this project. At first we were reluctant to say anything more than that we are here because of God's love. Then as we gradually came to know people, hungering for more fellowship ourselves, we sought after Rafael and established the weekly worship.

Now a morning prayer and Scripture group meets six days a week. Through this setting, we are getting to know those with whom we work and

November, Week four

Baß Son Jose

are being known. This morning we prayed for Feliz' wife who is having fever after the birth of their third child. Faye and I were able to visit her on the way home and pray with her. Then we looked up her symptoms in the book, *Where There Is No Doctor*. At lunchtime Jim took the nurse to see her with penicillin a doctor friend had donated.

It is a teaching by living together, by sharing what we have, and receiving.

My child,

I touch you so that I can touch others through you. You are Mine and there are others I have called, but they are not listening. So I use you as My hands and feet, My heart, to get their attention. Your joy is made full to overflowing by being useful in My plan.

" . . . Christ in you, the hope of glory: Whom we preach, warning every man, and teaching every man in all wisdom; that we may present every man perfect in Christ Jesus."

Colossians 1:27–28, KJV

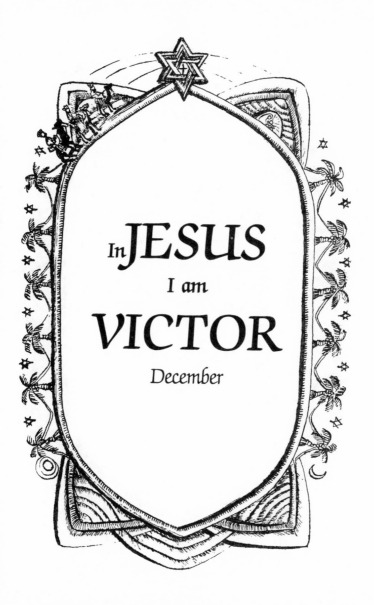

In JESUS
I am
VICTOR

December

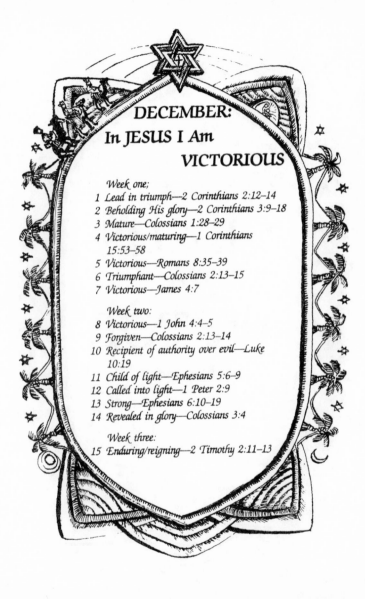

DECEMBER:

In JESUS I Am

VICTORIOUS

Week one;
1 *Lead in triumph—2 Corinthians 2:12–14*
2 *Beholding His glory—2 Corinthians 3:9–18*
3 *Mature—Colossians 1:28–29*
4 *Victorious/maturing—1 Corinthians 15:53–58*
5 *Victorious—Romans 8:35–39*
6 *Triumphant—Colossians 2:13–15*
7 *Victorious—James 4:7*

Week two:
8 *Victorious—1 John 4:4–5*
9 *Forgiven—Colossians 2:13–14*
10 *Recipient of authority over evil—Luke 10:19*
11 *Child of light—Ephesians 5:6–9*
12 *Called into light—1 Peter 2:9*
13 *Strong—Ephesians 6:10–19*
14 *Revealed in glory—Colossians 3:4*

Week three:
15 *Enduring/reigning—2 Timothy 2:11–13*

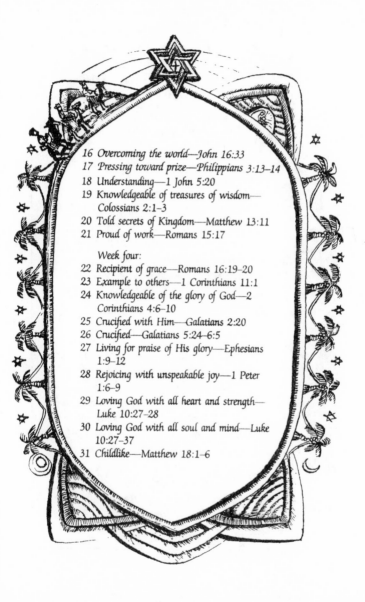

16 *Overcoming the world—John 16:33*

17 *Pressing toward prize—Philippians 3:13–14*

18 *Understanding—1 John 5:20*

19 *Knowledgeable of treasures of wisdom—Colossians 2:1–3*

20 *Told secrets of Kingdom—Matthew 13:11*

21 *Proud of work—Romans 15:17*

Week four:

22 *Recipient of grace—Romans 16:19–20*

23 *Example to others—1 Corinthians 11:1*

24 *Knowledgeable of the glory of God—2 Corinthians 4:6–10*

25 *Crucified with Him—Galatians 2:20*

26 *Crucified—Galatians 5:24–6:5*

27 *Living for praise of His glory—Ephesians 1:9–12*

28 *Rejoicing with unspeakable joy—1 Peter 1:6–9*

29 *Loving God with all heart and strength—Luke 10:27–28*

30 *Loving God with all soul and mind—Luke 10:27–37*

31 *Childlike—Matthew 18:1–6*

In JESUS God leads me in TRIUMPH

The procession has begun. God has triumphed over hostile, supernatural forces. The enemy is slain; the conqueror rejoices.

I woke with a vivid, gradually unfolding picture in my mind, and after breakfast I sat down and began sketching. As the figures took shape, Celestino, Santiago, and Rafael watched. They were each in the picture of the "new Nicaragua, a new Eden."

Celestino and Santiago laughed when they saw they were hanging from a tree by a loop in a serpent's tail made of woman's hair and *guado*, white lightning. Unused and covered with cobwebs were their swords of the Spirit. Rafael, in the picture, was smiling up at the long hair, caressing it. He did not see the serpent's leering face almost touching his. Sword in hand, but unaware of the danger, Rafael could not deal with the forces of evil adequately.

December, Week one

Rafael did not laugh at this picture.
We talked about it at length. I believe
the Lord used this unusual method to
wake us all to the reality of evil here,
to urge us to take the authority He
has given and to walk victoriously.

Father, I know that You are Victor,
but my focus is not always on You,
so I slip into unbelief.

My child,

be patient. Seek only to be with Me,
and you will see that the enemy is
vanquished, his dread power bound by
chains.

"Now thanks be unto God which
always causeth us to triumph in
Christ, and maketh manifest the savor
of his knowledge by us in every
place."

2 Corinthians 2:14, KJV

In JESUS I see GOD'S GLORY

The veil lifted. The covering over the glory and presence of the Lord God is removed, completely done away with.

Moses had to wear a veil because the reflected glory of God on his face was too strong for the people to look upon. Now in the Messiah Jesus, the veil is removed. Spiritually blind eyes are opened to see the splendor and magnificent radiance of God.

Father, I know that on the Cross Jesus tore the veil of the Holy of Holies. Even I have seen Your brightness and know that within Jesus was Your glory. Father, so many still are in darkness. They even ridicule me or look on me with contempt for this love of You. Isn't this glory for them too?

December, Week two

My child,

when you have once seen, you cannot deny.
When you have seen Me, My radiance rests on
your face. People in darkness will see this and be
drawn as moths to light. Keep in that place
where you can see Me, and say with Stephen,
"Father, forgive them."

"But their minds were blinded: for until this day
remaineth the same veil untaken away" in the
reading of the old testament; which veil is done
away in Christ. . . . But we all, with open face,
beholding as in a glass the glory of the Lord, are
changed into the same image from glory to glory,
even as by the Spirit of the Lord."

2 Corinthians 3:14–15, 18, KJV

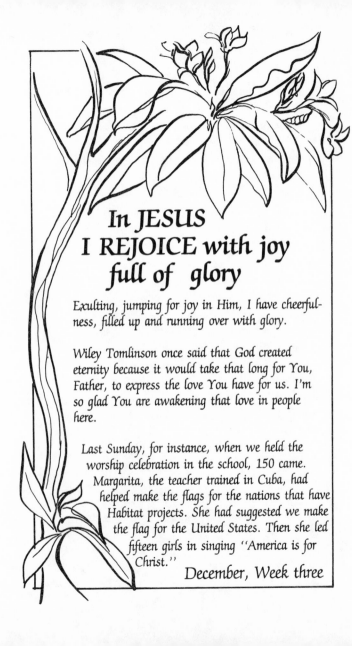

In JESUS
I REJOICE with joy
full of glory

Exulting, jumping for joy in Him, I have cheerfulness, filled up and running over with glory.

Wiley Tomlinson once said that God created eternity because it would take that long for You, Father, to express the love You have for us. I'm so glad You are awakening that love in people here.

Last Sunday, for instance, when we held the worship celebration in the school, 150 came. Margarita, the teacher trained in Cuba, had helped make the flags for the nations that have Habitat projects. She had suggested we make the flag for the United States. Then she led fifteen girls in singing "America is for Christ."

December, Week three

I keep looking ahead, knowing that we will leave here. The seeds of the Word are being steadily planted. Yet I am warned by what happened to our garden: Birds, chickens, pigs, and even cows got in and ate every single tender plant.

We must work to build fences around this garden, to protect these young plants from destructive forces. I feel the urgency. . . .

My child,

when your time to be separated from them comes, it will be sorrowful because you will be parted for a time, but the joy is greatest because you have found something together, the unity of the Spirit, which nothing and no one can take away—it is eternal joy.

"And now come I to thee; and these things I speak in the world, that they might have my joy fulfilled in themselves."

John 17:13, KJV

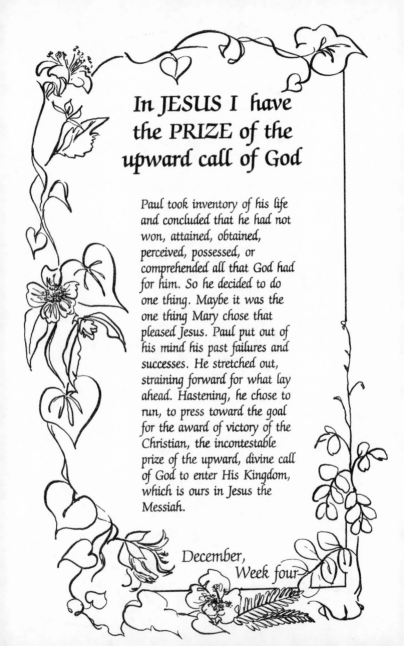

In JESUS I have the PRIZE of the upward call of God

Paul took inventory of his life and concluded that he had not won, attained, obtained, perceived, possessed, or comprehended all that God had for him. So he decided to do one thing. Maybe it was the one thing Mary chose that pleased Jesus. Paul put out of his mind his past failures and successes. He stretched out, straining forward for what lay ahead. Hastening, he chose to run, to press toward the goal for the award of victory of the Christian, the incontestable prize of the upward, divine call of God to enter His Kingdom, which is ours in Jesus the Messiah.

December,
Week four

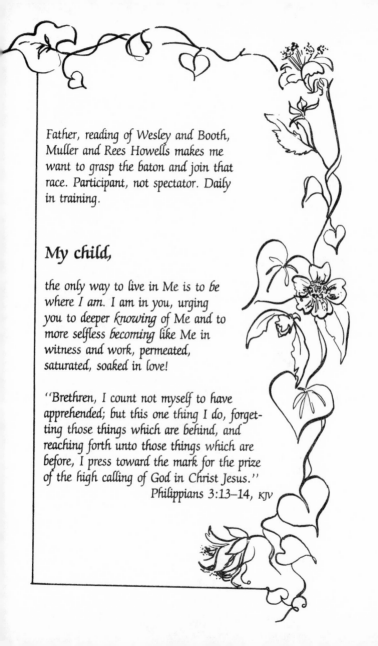

Father, reading of Wesley and Booth, Muller and Rees Howells makes me want to grasp the baton and join that race. Participant, not spectator. Daily in training.

My child,

the only way to live in Me is to be where *I am*. I am in you, urging you to deeper *knowing* of Me and to more selfless *becoming* like Me in witness and work, permeated, saturated, soaked in love!

''Brethren, I count not myself to have apprehended; but this one thing I do, forgetting those things which are behind, and reaching forth unto those things which are before, I press toward the mark for the prize of the high calling of God in Christ Jesus.''

Philippians 3:13–14, KJV

If Jesus is our righteousness, then no human is
      better or worse than me.
If we fight not against flesh and blood, but
      against spiritual forces and principalities,
      then no human is my enemy.
If God is my provision, then I don't need to lay
      up treasures on earth or defensively hoard
      and protect my possessions.
If God is our creator, then every human is worth
      knowing, and respecting, and serving as a
      beautiful, unique, amazing example of
      God's love and creativity, no matter how
      poor or socially different from me.
If God is my protector, I do not need to be afraid
      of any change, or any person, or any
      circumstance.
If God is my forgiveness, I do not need to be
      afraid of stumbling or falling;
Besides, He does not give us fear and timidity,
      but love, power, and clear thinking.

Jim Hornsby, August 1985
German Pomares, Nicaragua